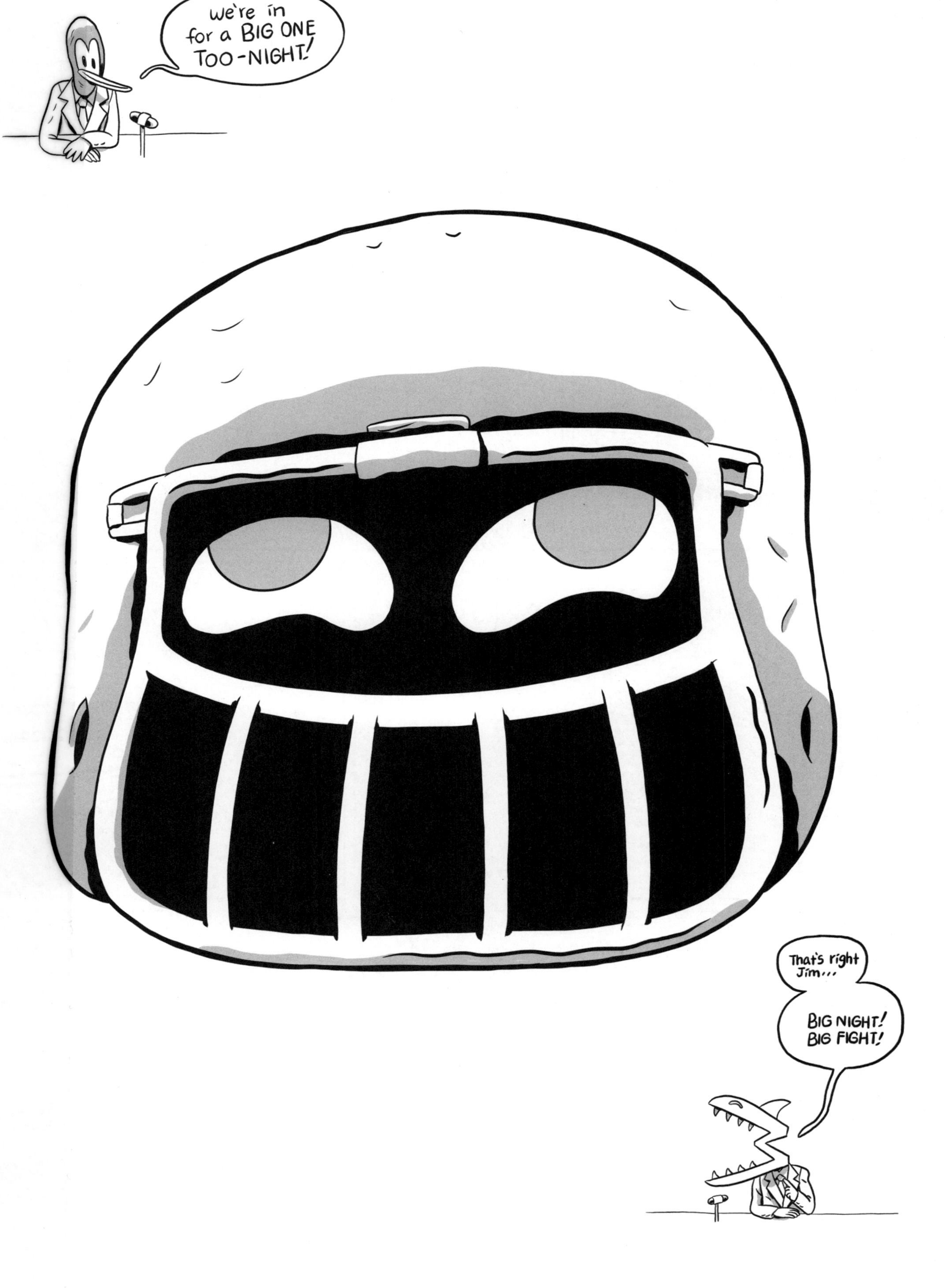
We're in for a BIG ONE TOO-NIGHT!
That's right Jim...
BIG NIGHT! BIG FIGHT!

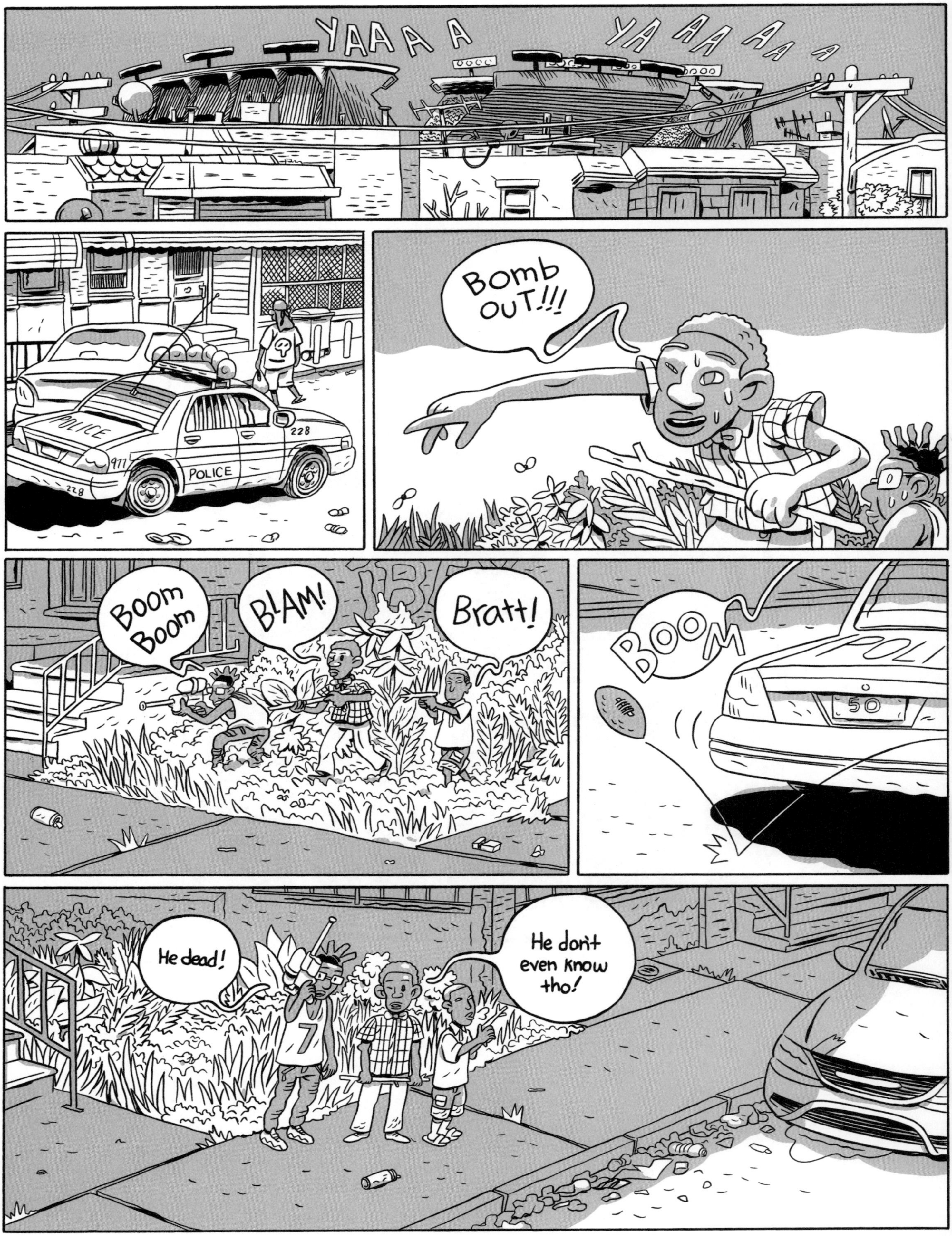
YAAAA A
YA AAAAA A
Bomb OUT!!!!
Boom Boom
BLAM!
Bratt!
BOOM
He dead!
He don't even know tho!

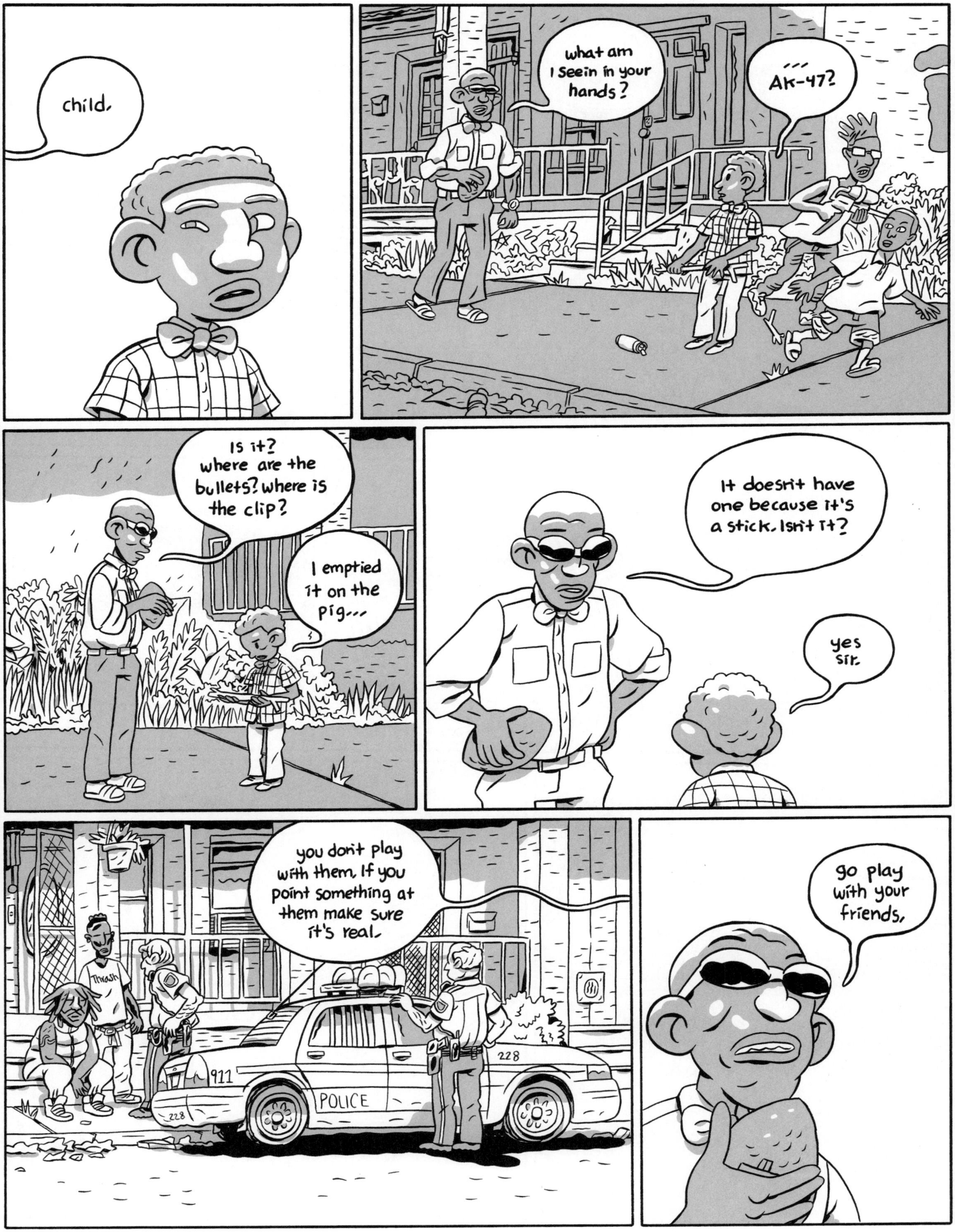
child,
what am I seein in your hands?
... Ak-47?
Is it? where are the bullets? where is the clip?
I emptied it on the pig...
It doesn't have one because it's a stick. Isn't it?
yes sir.
you don't play with them. If you point something at them make sure it's real.
Thrash
911
228
POLICE
228
228
go play with your friends.

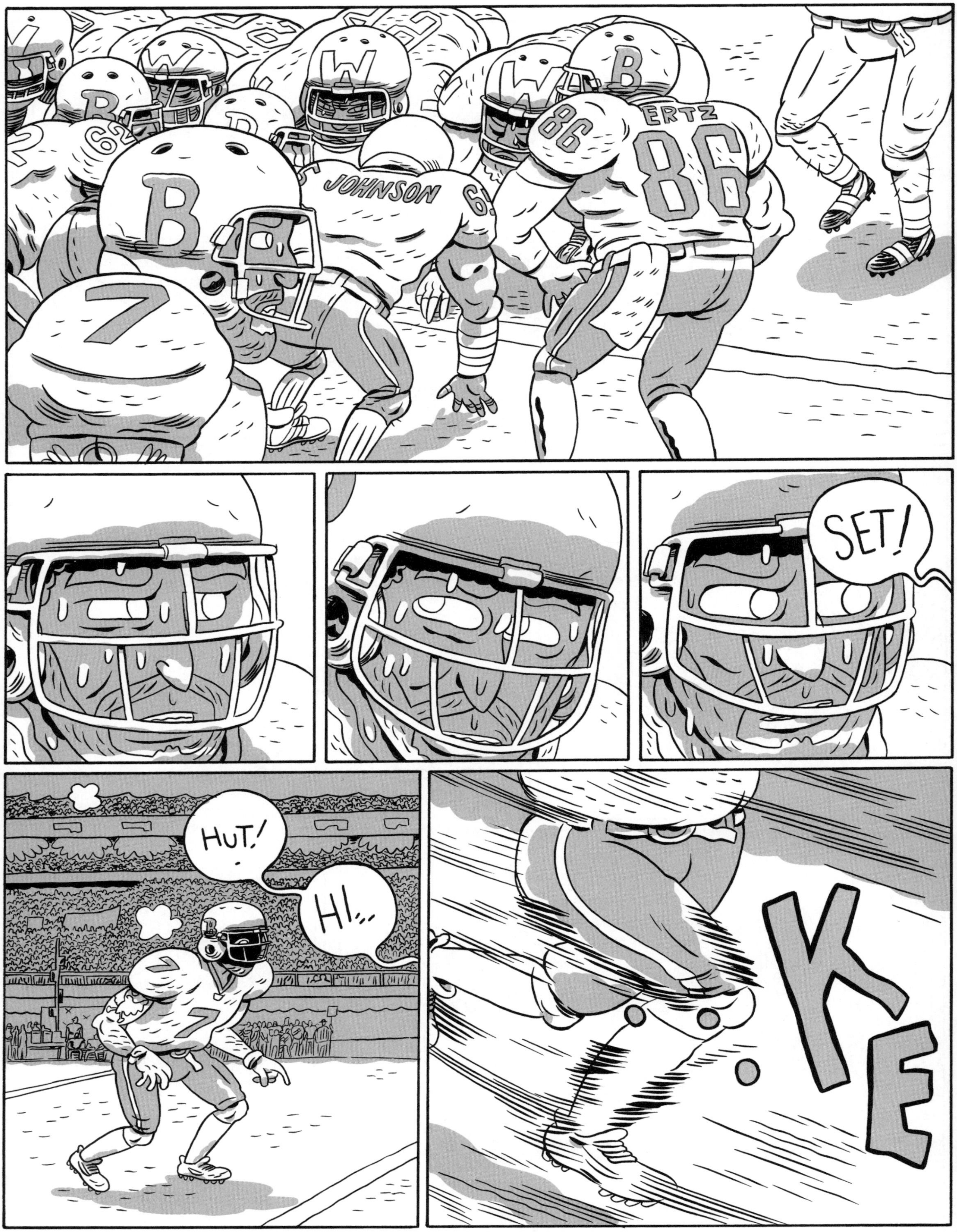

JOHNSON
ERTZ
SET!
HUT!
HI...
KE

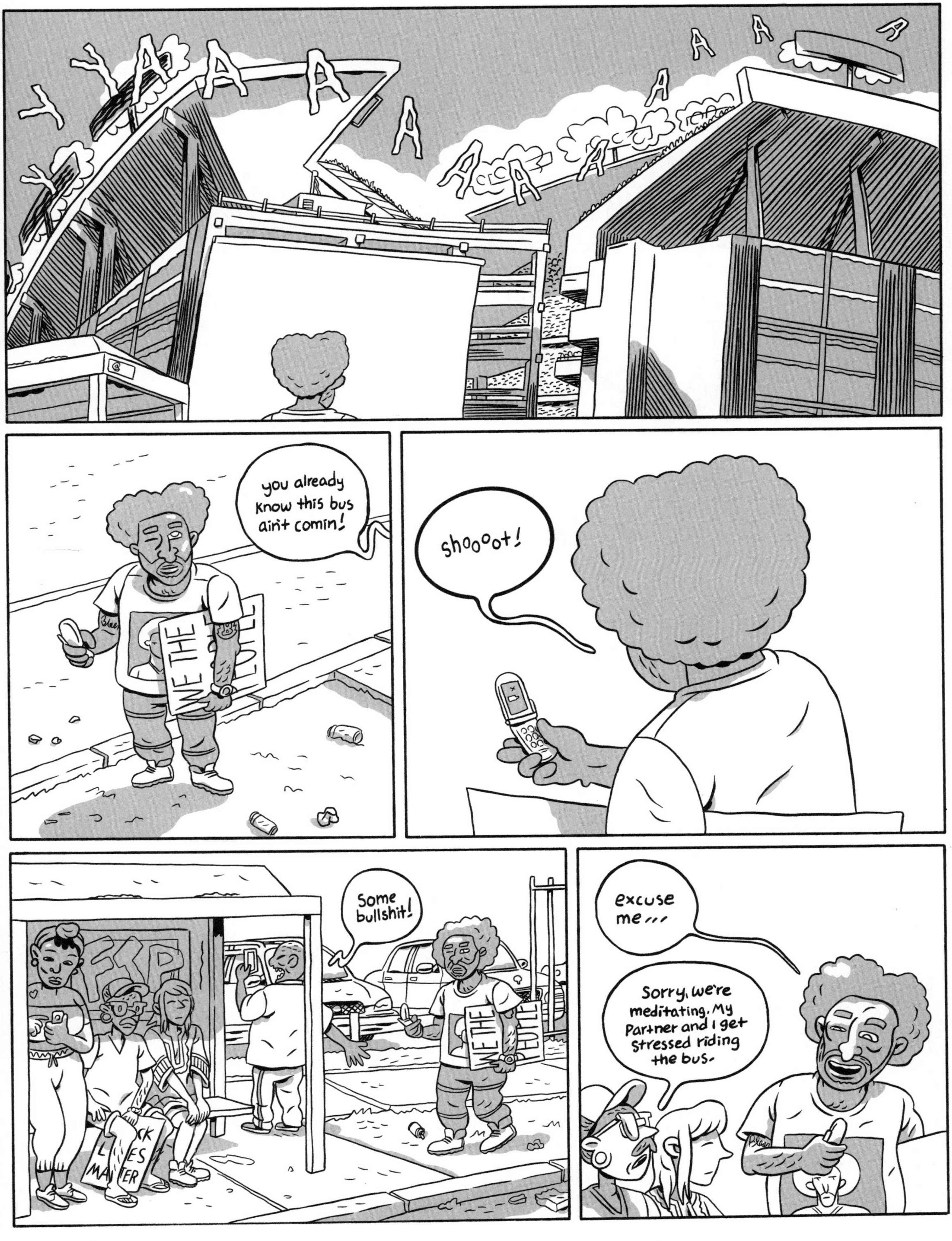
YYAAAAAAAAAAAA
you already know this bus ain't comin!
WE THE PEOPLE
shoooot!
Some bullshit!
WE THE PEOPLE
excuse me...
Sorry, we're meditating. My Partner and I get stressed riding the bus.

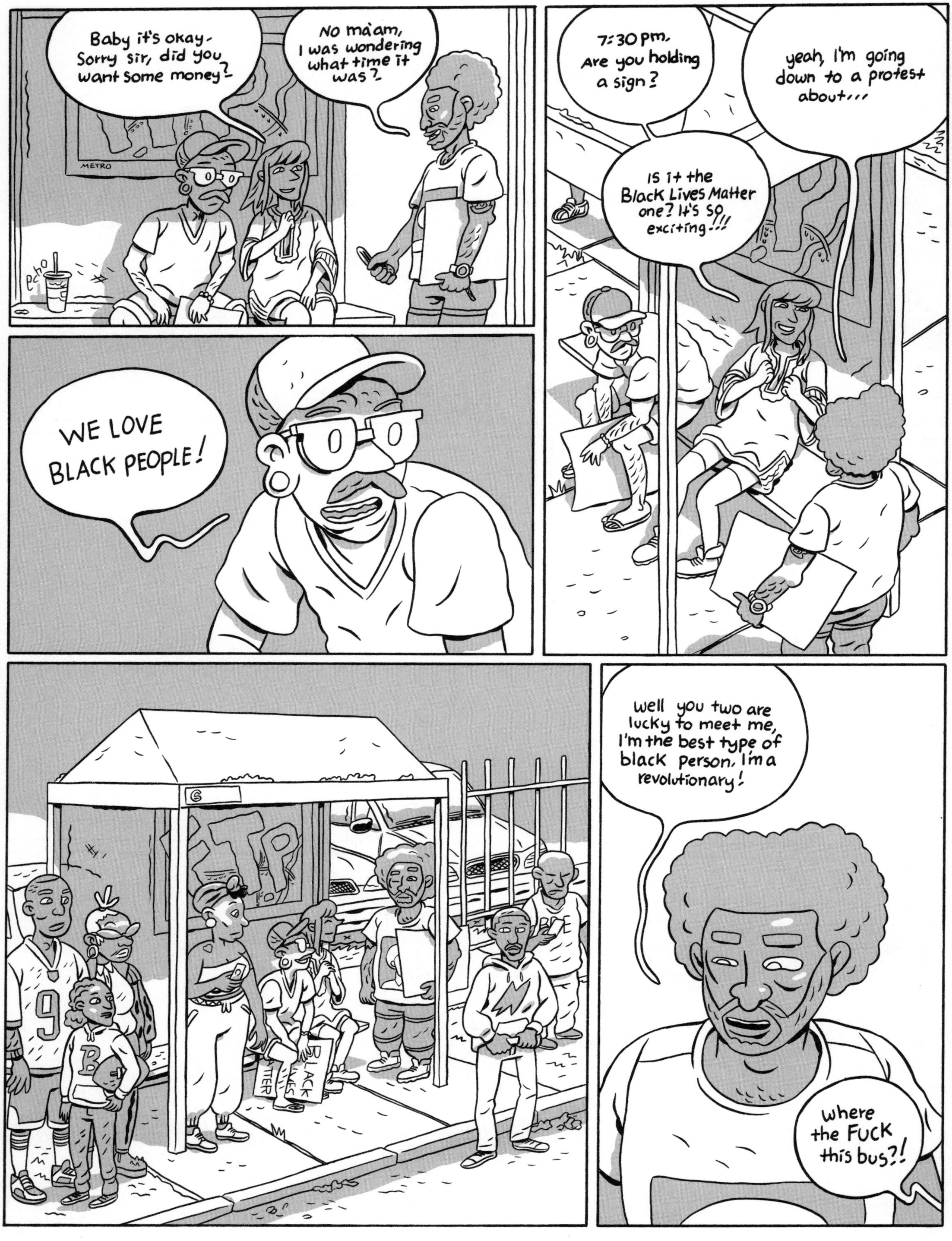
Baby it's okay- Sorry sir, did you want some money?
No ma'am, I was wondering what time it was?
METRO
7:30 pm, Are you holding a sign?
yeah, I'm going down to a protest about...
Is it the Black Lives Matter one? It's so exciting!!!
WE LOVE BLACK PEOPLE!
Well you two are lucky to meet me, I'm the best type of black person, I'm a revolutionary!
where the FUCK this bus?!

tonight we'll see if very controversial wide receiver Marshall Quandary Collins will play! What do you think his chances are Thomas?

He really shot himself in the foot getting all political this early in his career, I don't think he'll have a place in football after this season.

But what if he plays well? At this point he's known for his stance against police brutality much more than his ball playing.

End of the day he's bad for any team's brand even if he performs well tonight.

Last week he really riled up football fans when he made an inflammatory statement during an interview.

Do you intend to kneel during the national anthem, despite many people calling it disrespectful?

yes.

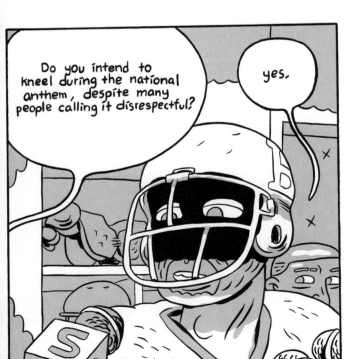

very shocking.

Let's see what Twitter is saying.

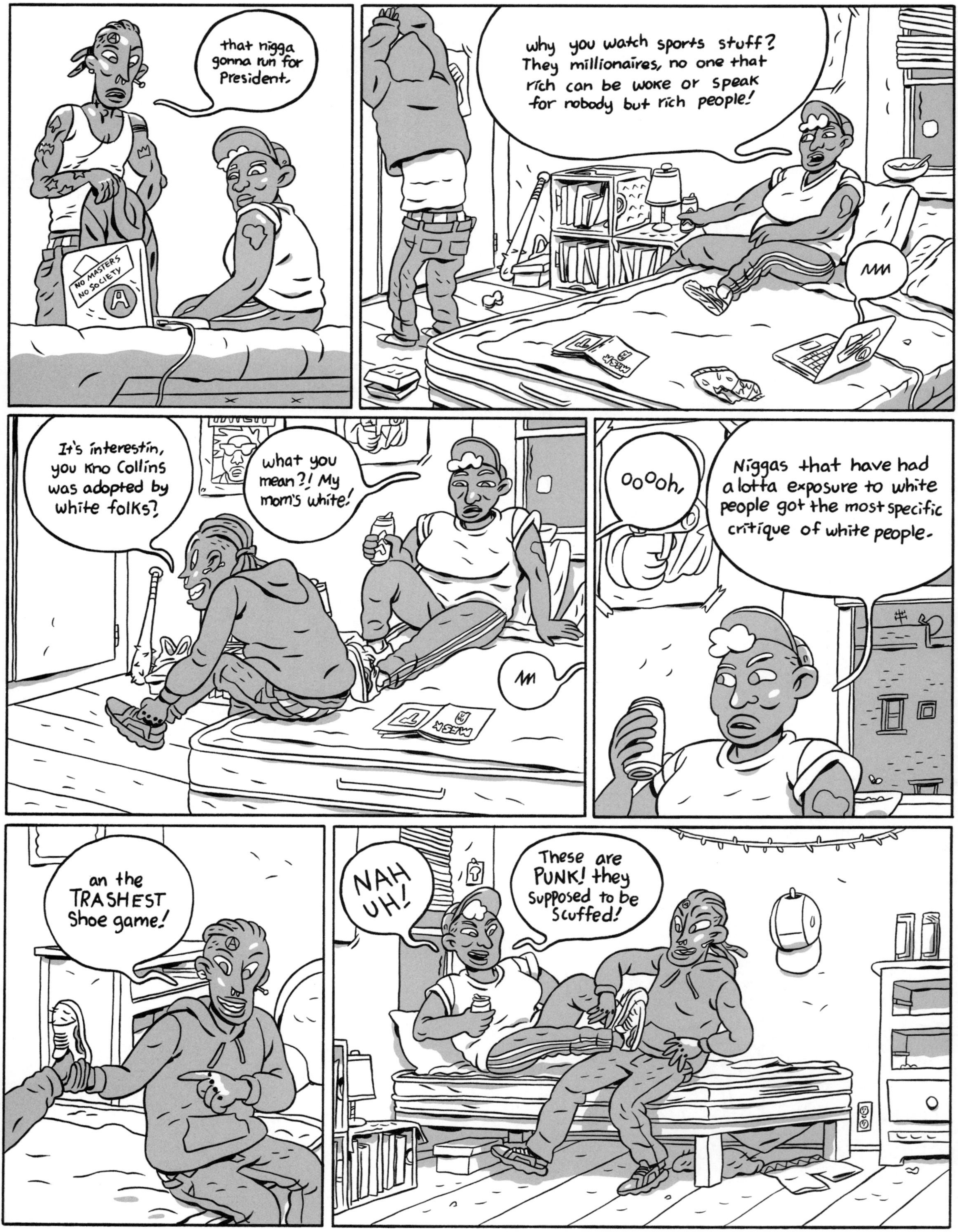

that nigga gonna run for President.
NO MASTERS NO SOCIETY
why you watch sports stuff? They millionaires, no one that rich can be woke or speak for nobody but rich people!
It's interestin, you kno Collins was adopted by white folks?
what you mean?! My mom's white!
Ooooh,
Niggas that have had a lotta exposure to white people got the most specific critique of white people.
an the TRASHEST Shoe game!
NAH UH!
These are PUNK! they supposed to be Scuffed!

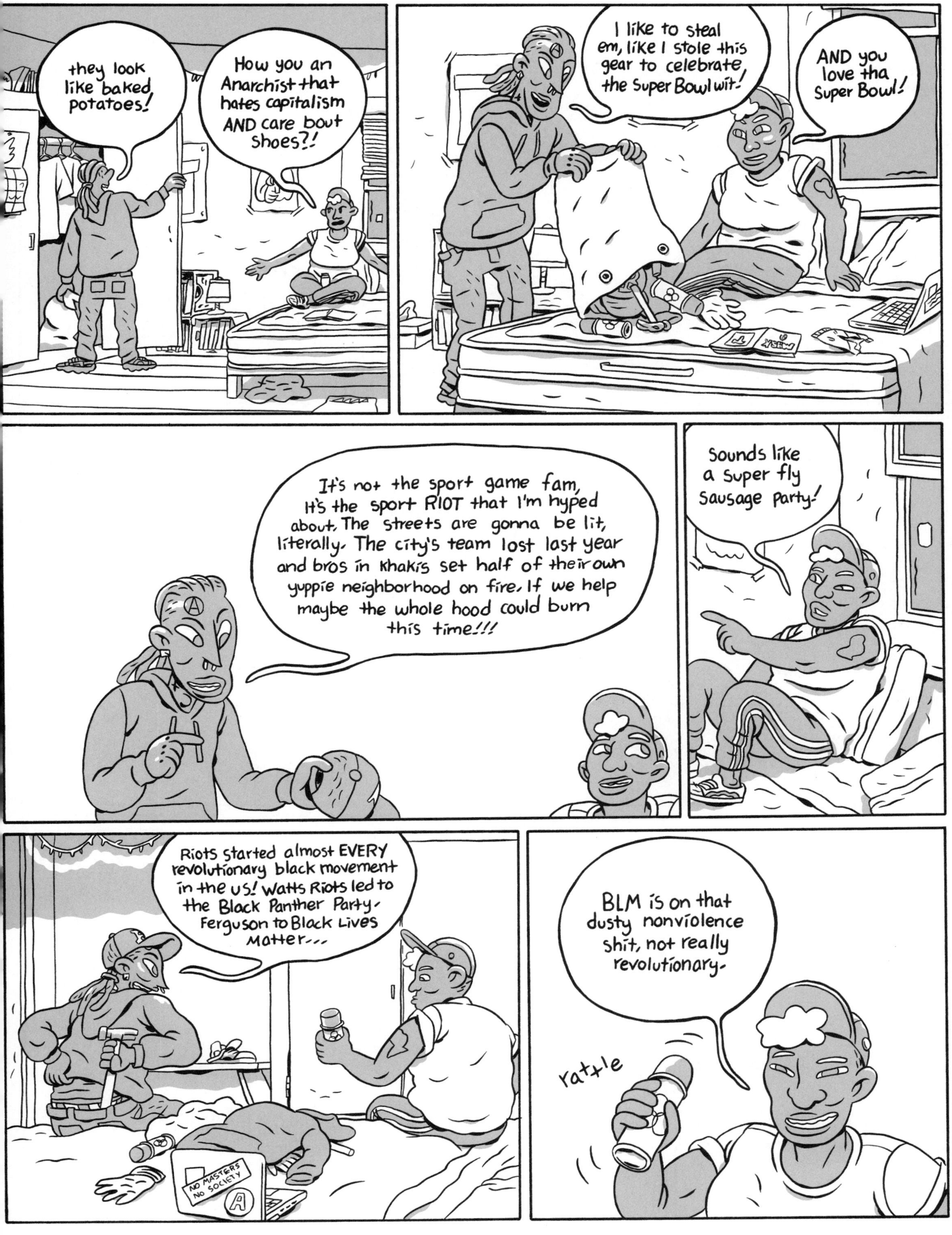
they look like baked potatoes!
How you an Anarchist that hates capitalism AND care bout shoes?!
I like to steal em, like I stole this gear to celebrate the Super Bowl wit!
AND you love tha Super Bowl!
It's not the sport game fam, It's the sport RIOT that I'm hyped about. The streets are gonna be lit, literally. The city's team lost last year and bros in khakis set half of their own yuppie neighborhood on fire. If we help maybe the whole hood could burn this time!!!
Sounds like a super fly sausage party!
Riots started almost EVERY revolutionary black movement in the US! Watts Riots led to the Black Panther Party. Ferguson to Black Lives Matter...
NO MASTERS NO SOCIETY
BLM is on that dusty nonviolence shit, not really revolutionary.
rattle

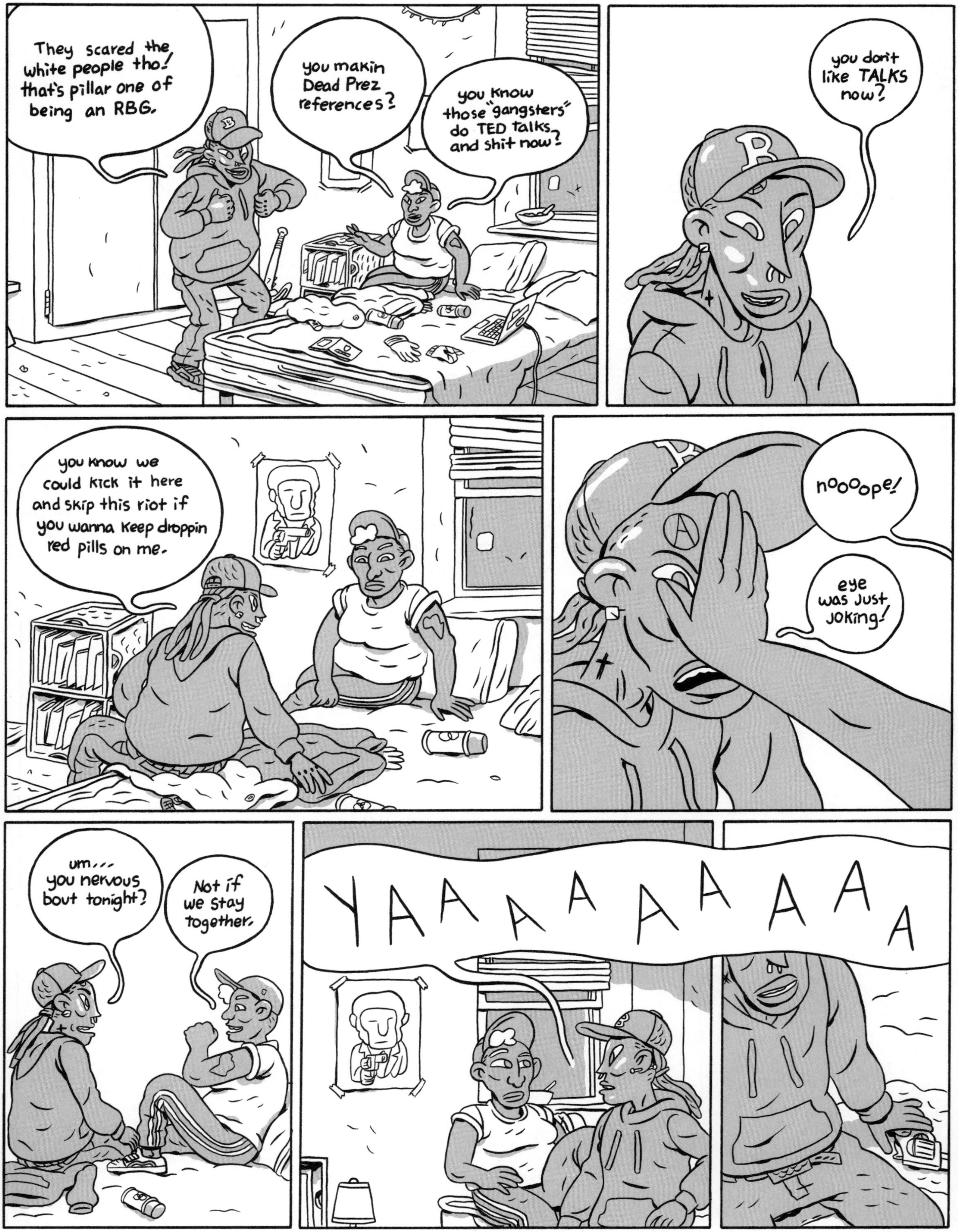
They scared the white people tho! that's pillar one of being an RBG.
you makin Dead Prez references?
you know those "gangsters" do TED talks and shit now?
you don't like TALKS now?
you know we could kick it here and skip this riot if you wanna keep droppin red pills on me.
nooooope!
eye was just joking!
um...
you nervous bout tonight?
Not if we stay together.
YAAAAAAAAAA

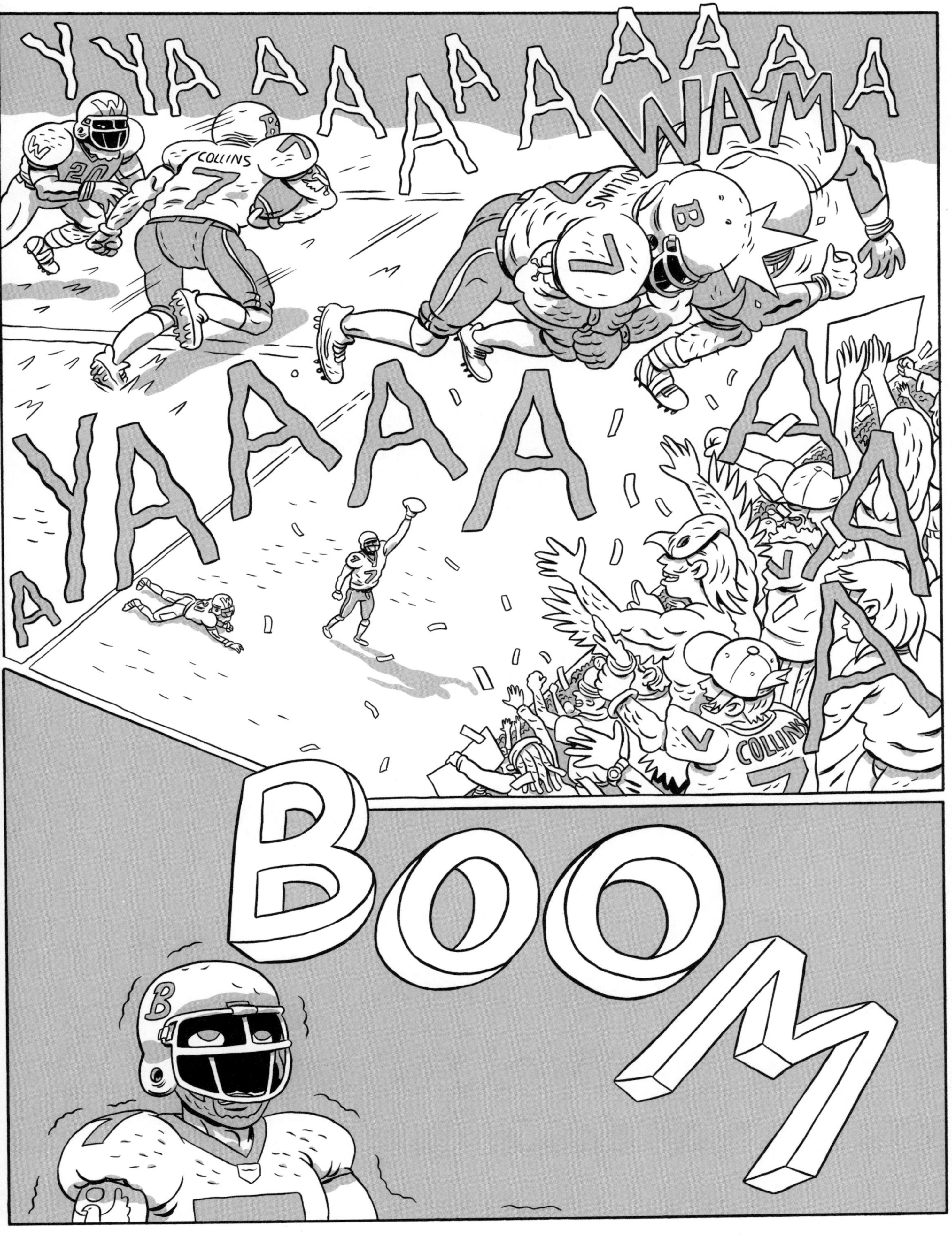

YYAAAAAAAAAAAA
COLLINS
7
WAM
YAAAAAAAA
COLLINS
BOOM

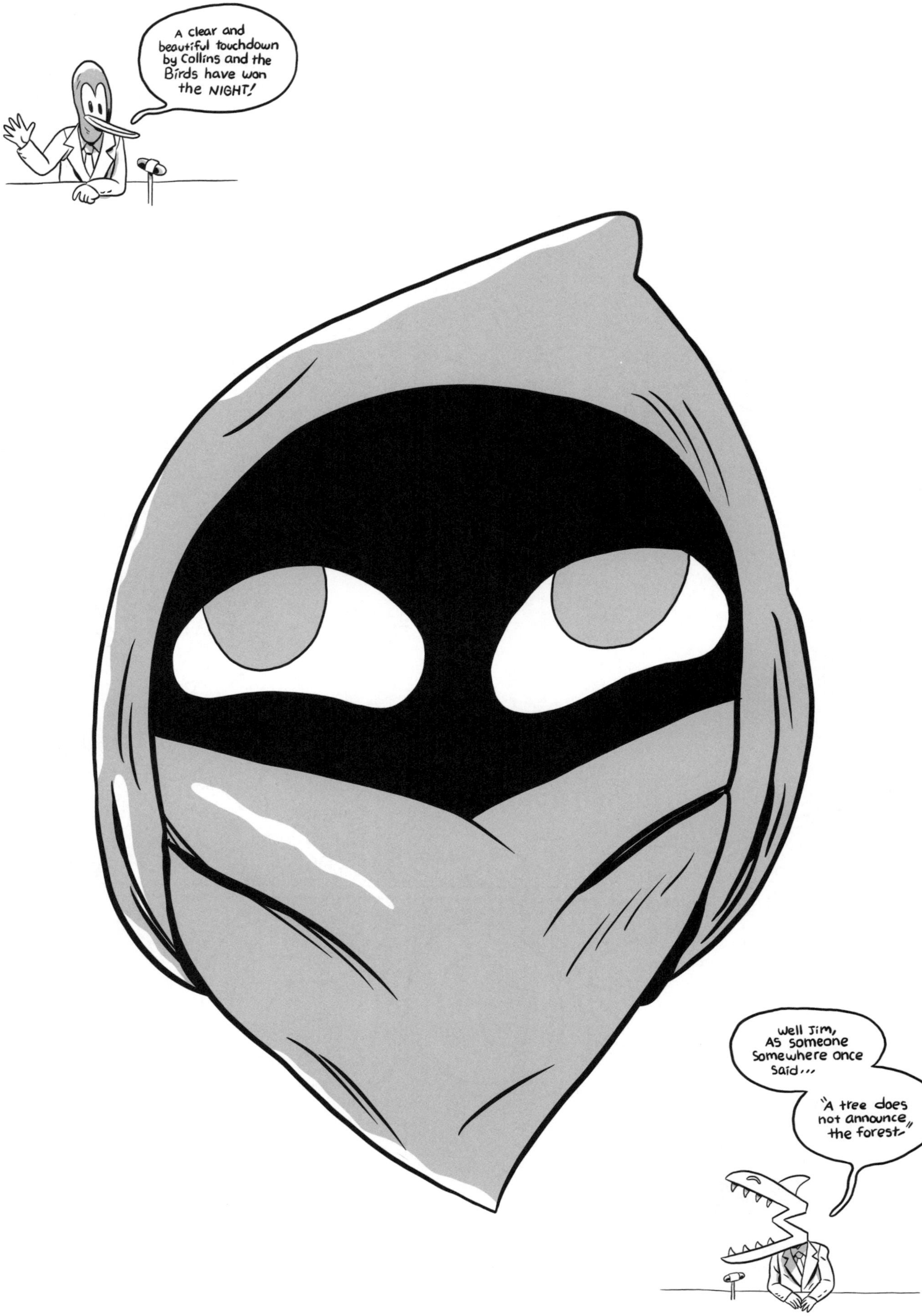
A clear and beautiful touchdown by Collins and the Birds have won the NIGHT!
Well Jim, AS someone Somewhere once said...
"A tree does not announce the forest."

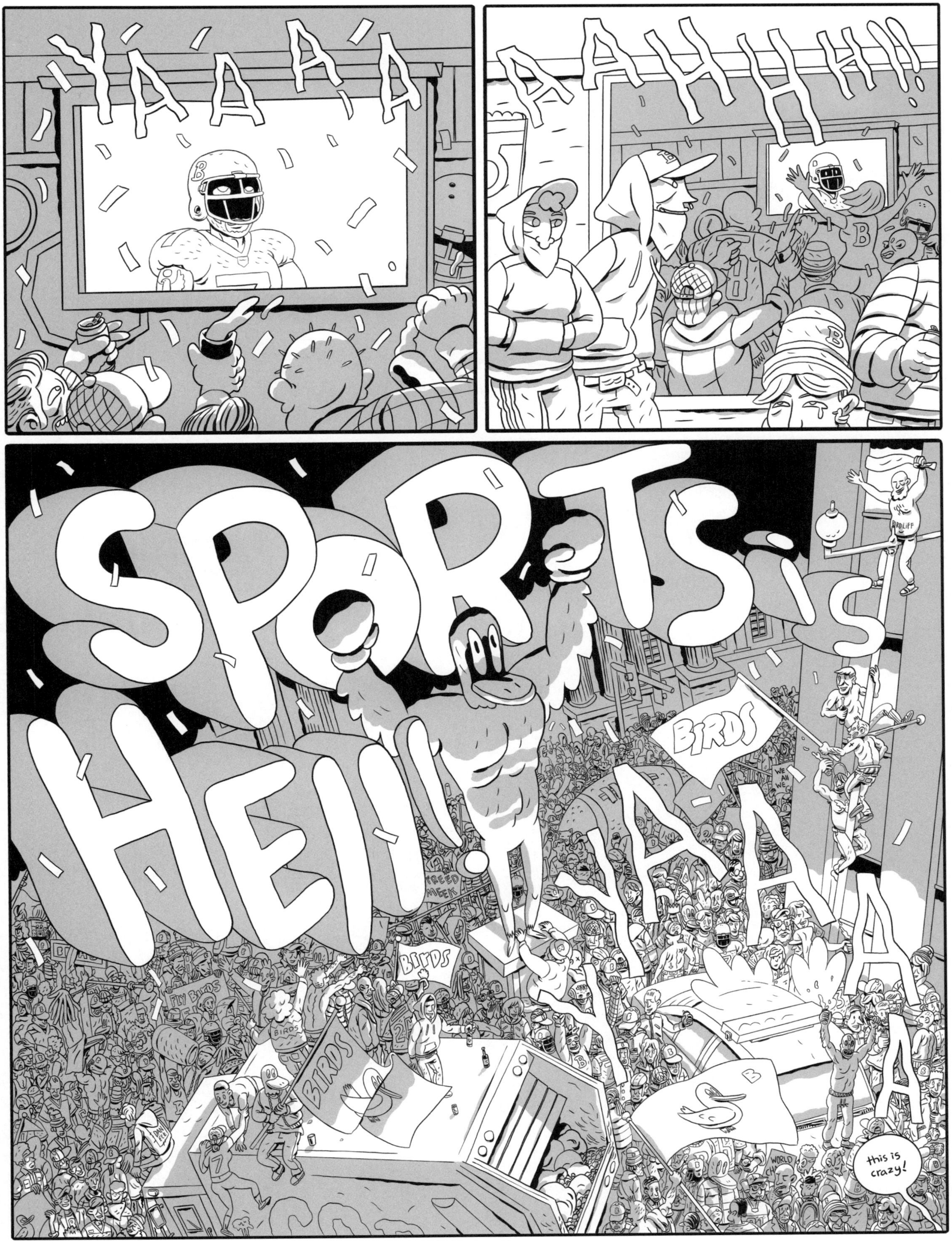

YAAAA
AAHHH!!
SPORTS IS HELL!
YAAAA
BIRDS
BIRDS
BIRDS
BIRDS
FLY BIRDS
this is crazy!

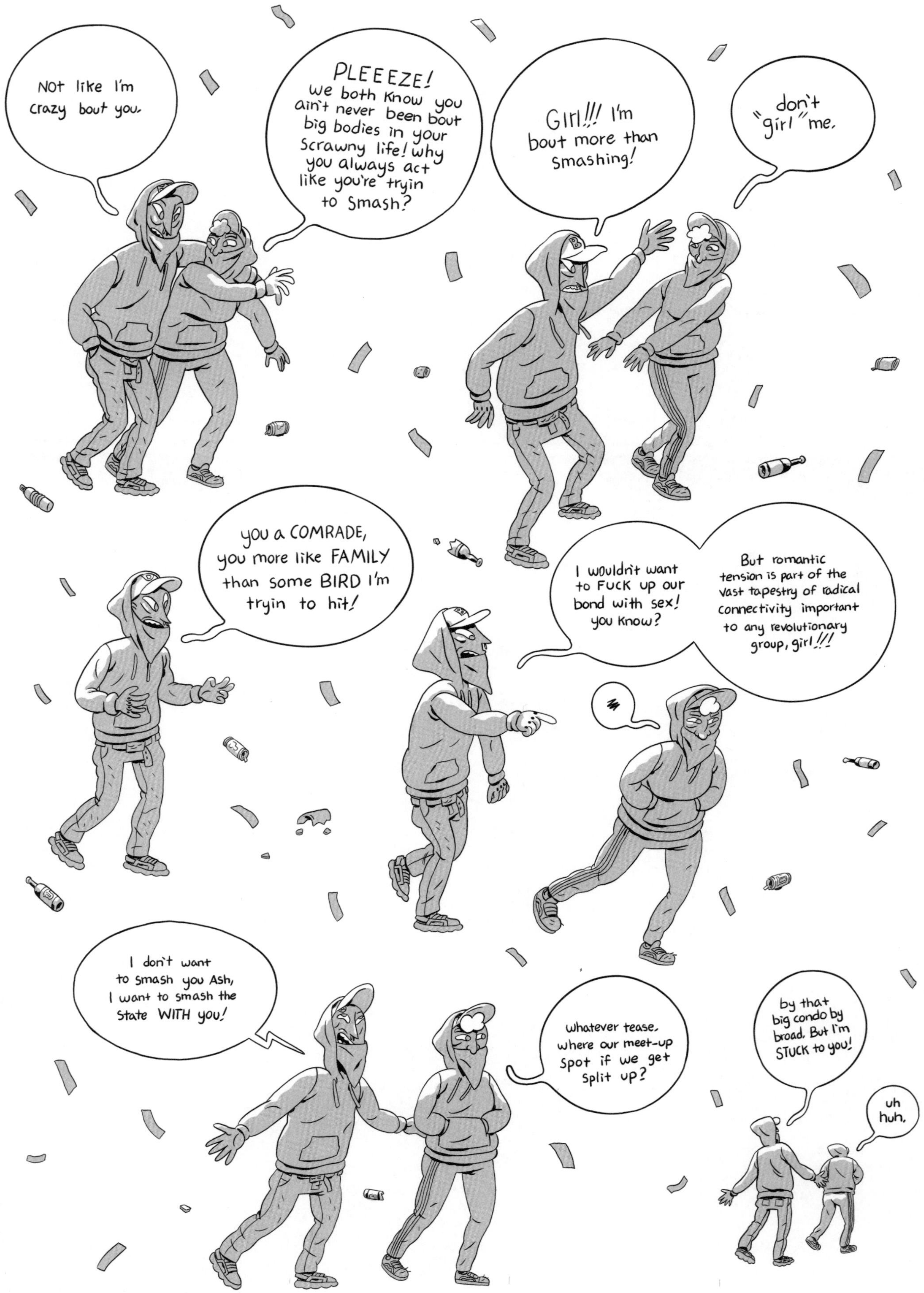
NOt like I'm crazy bout you.
PLEEEZE! we both Know you ain't never been bout big bodies in your Scrawny life! why you always act like you're tryin to Smash?
GIrl!!! I'm bout more than smashing!
don't "girl" me.
you a COMRADE, you more like FAMILY than some BIRD I'm tryin to hit!
I wouldn't want to FUCK up our bond with sex! you Know?
But romantic tension is part of the vast tapestry of radical connectivity important to any revolutionary group, girl!!!
I don't want to smash you Ash, I want to smash the State WITH you!
whatever tease. where our meet-up Spot if we get split up?
by that big condo by broad. But I'm STUCK to you!
uh huh.

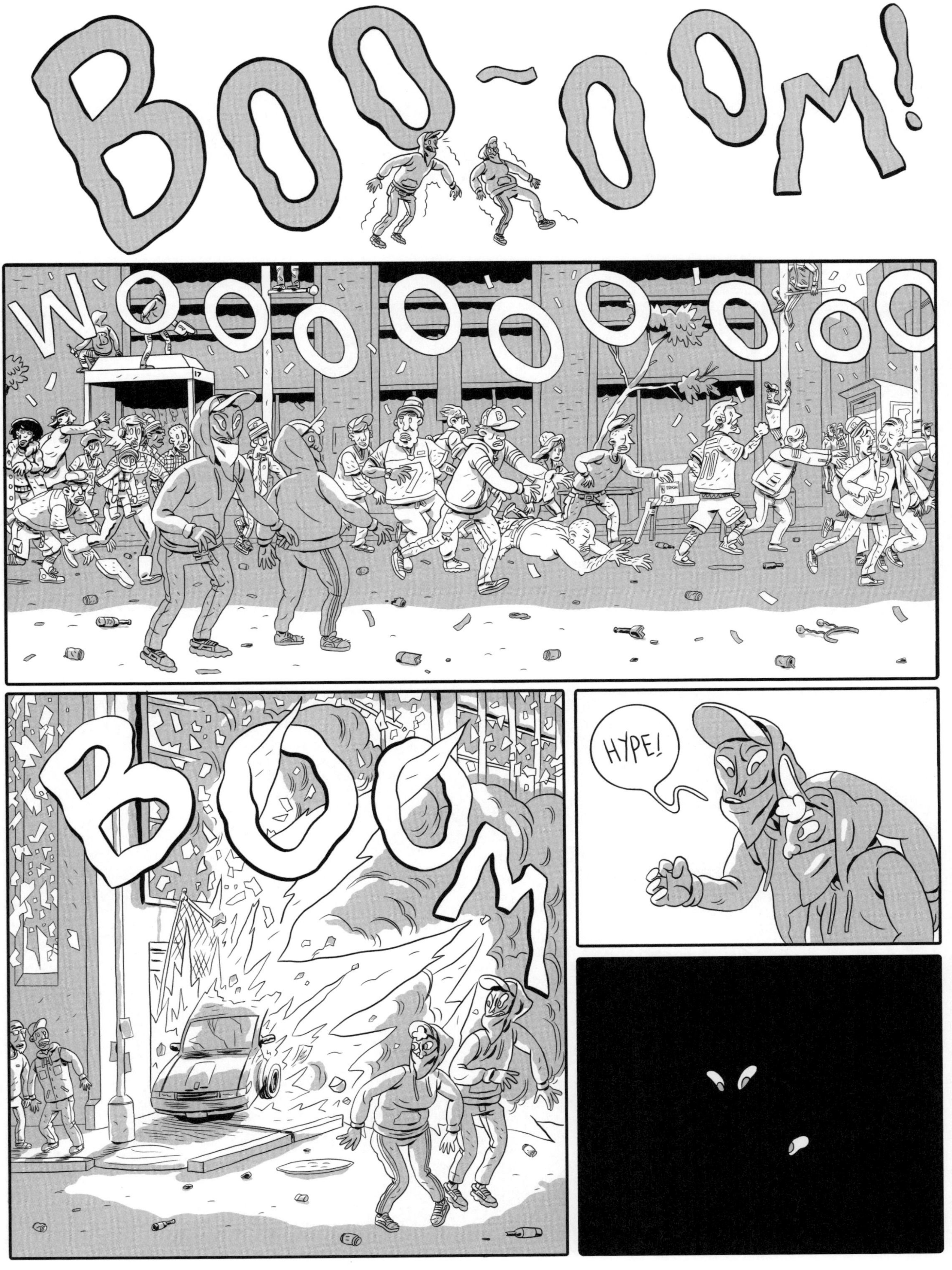
BOOO-OOOM!
WOOOOOOOOOO
BOOM
HYPE!

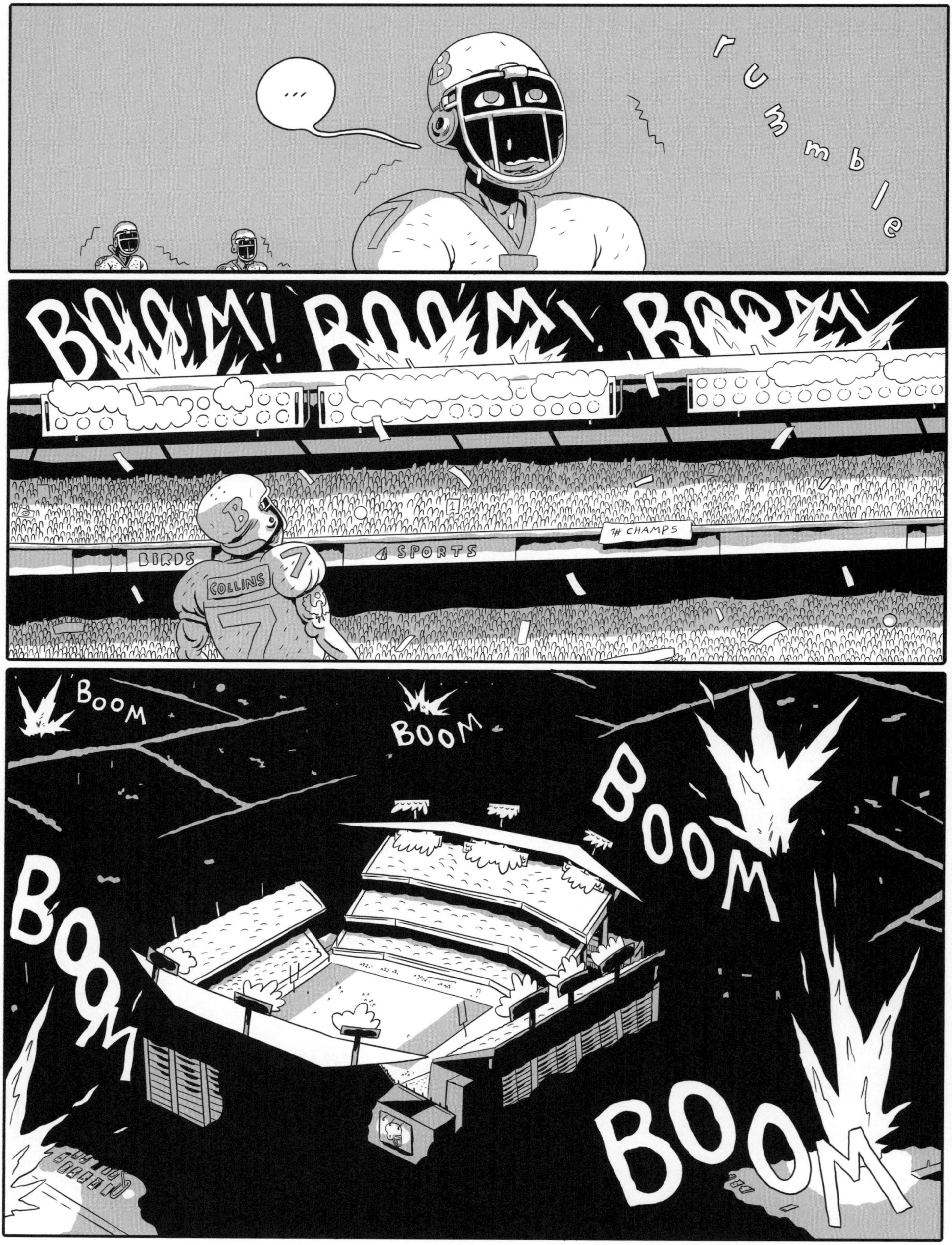
...
rumble
BOOM! BOOM! BOOM!
BIRDS
SPORTS
#1 CHAMPS
COLLINS
7
BOOM
BOOM
BOOM
BOOM
BOOM

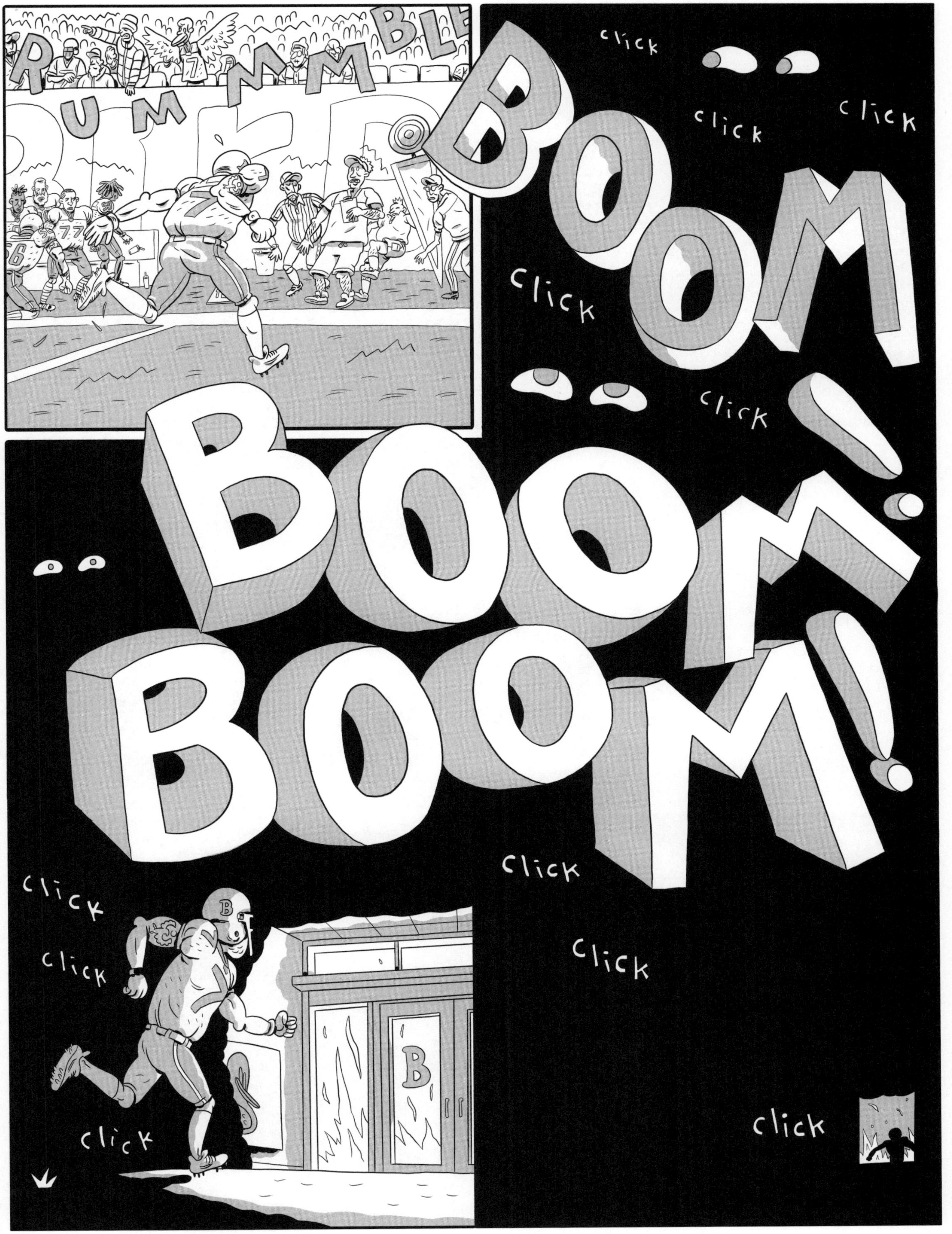
RUMMMBLE
click
BOOM
click
click
click
click
BOOM!
BOOM!
click
click
click
click
click
click

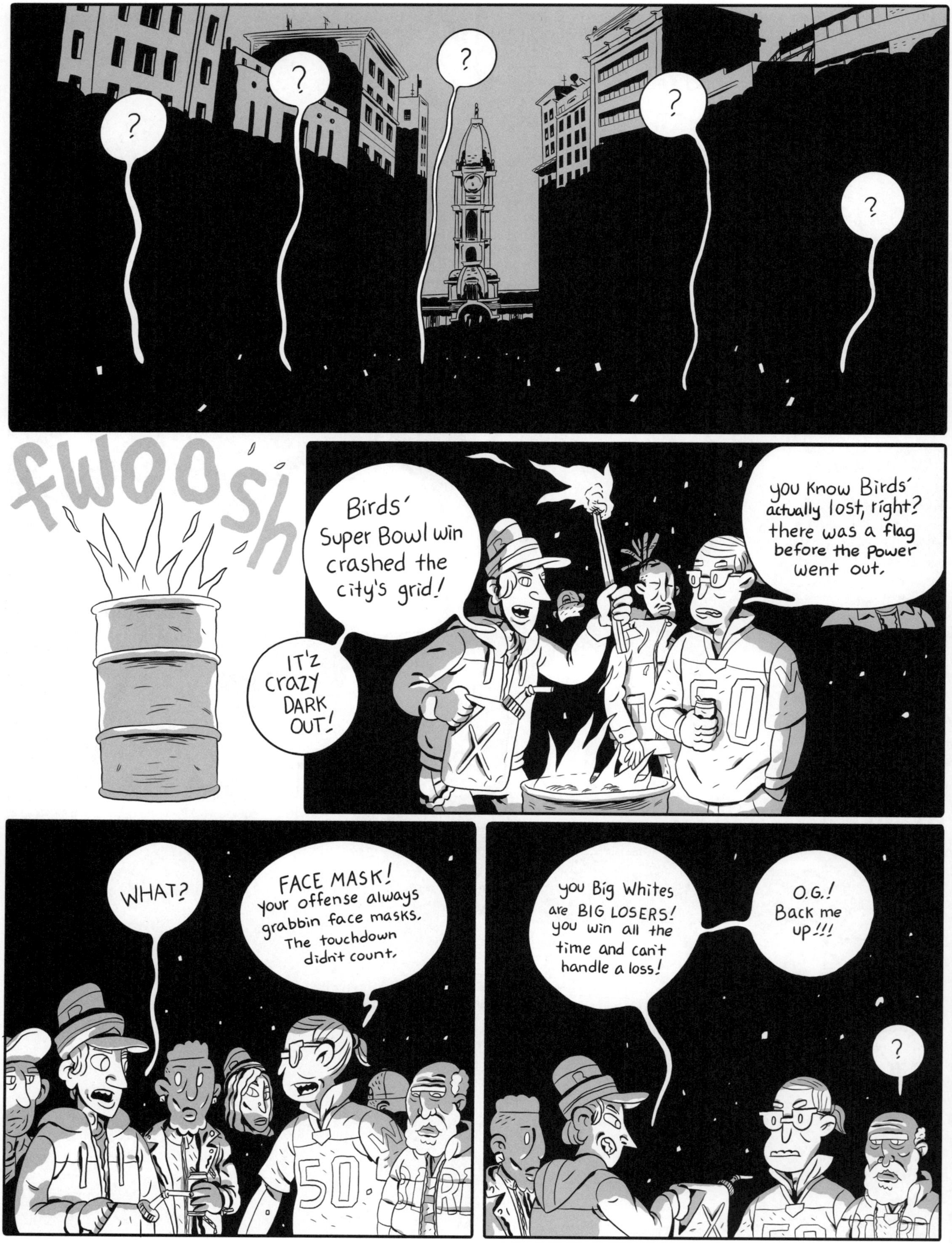
?
?
?
?
?
FWOOSH
Birds' Super Bowl win crashed the city's grid!
IT'Z crazy DARK OUT!
you know Birds' actually lost, right? there was a flag before the power went out.
WHAT?
FACE MASK! your offense always grabbin face masks. The touchdown didn't count.
you Big Whites are BIG LOSERS! you win all the time and can't handle a loss!
O.G.! Back me up!!!
?

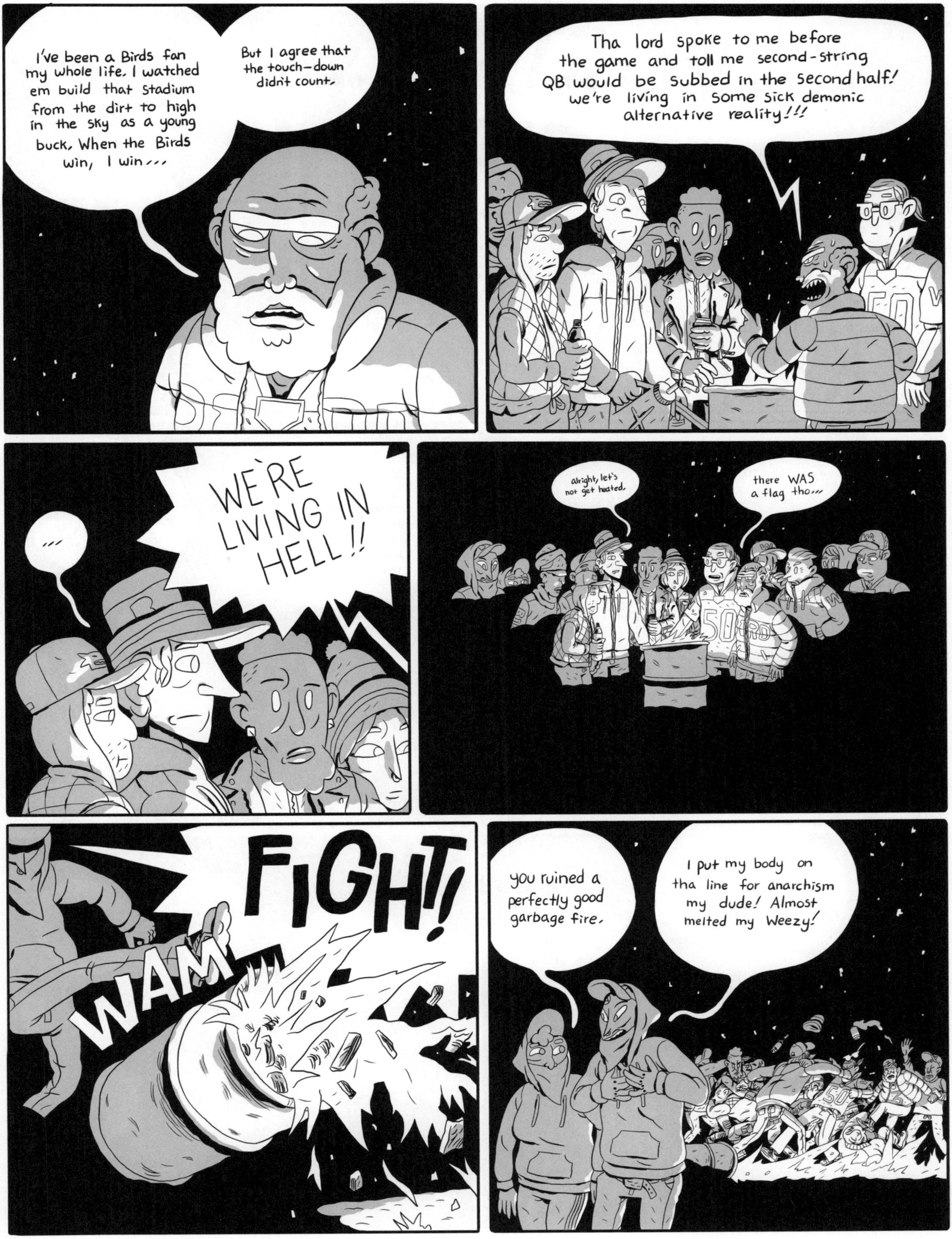

I've been a Birds fan my whole life. I watched em build that stadium from the dirt to high in the sky as a young buck. When the Birds win, I win...
But I agree that the touch-down didn't count.
Tha lord spoke to me before the game and toll me second-string QB would be subbed in the second half! we're living in some sick demonic alternative reality!!!
...
WE'RE LIVING IN HELL!!
alright, let's not get heated.
there WAS a flag tho...
FIGHT!!
WAM
you ruined a perfectly good garbage fire.
I put my body on tha line for anarchism my dude! Almost melted my Weezy!

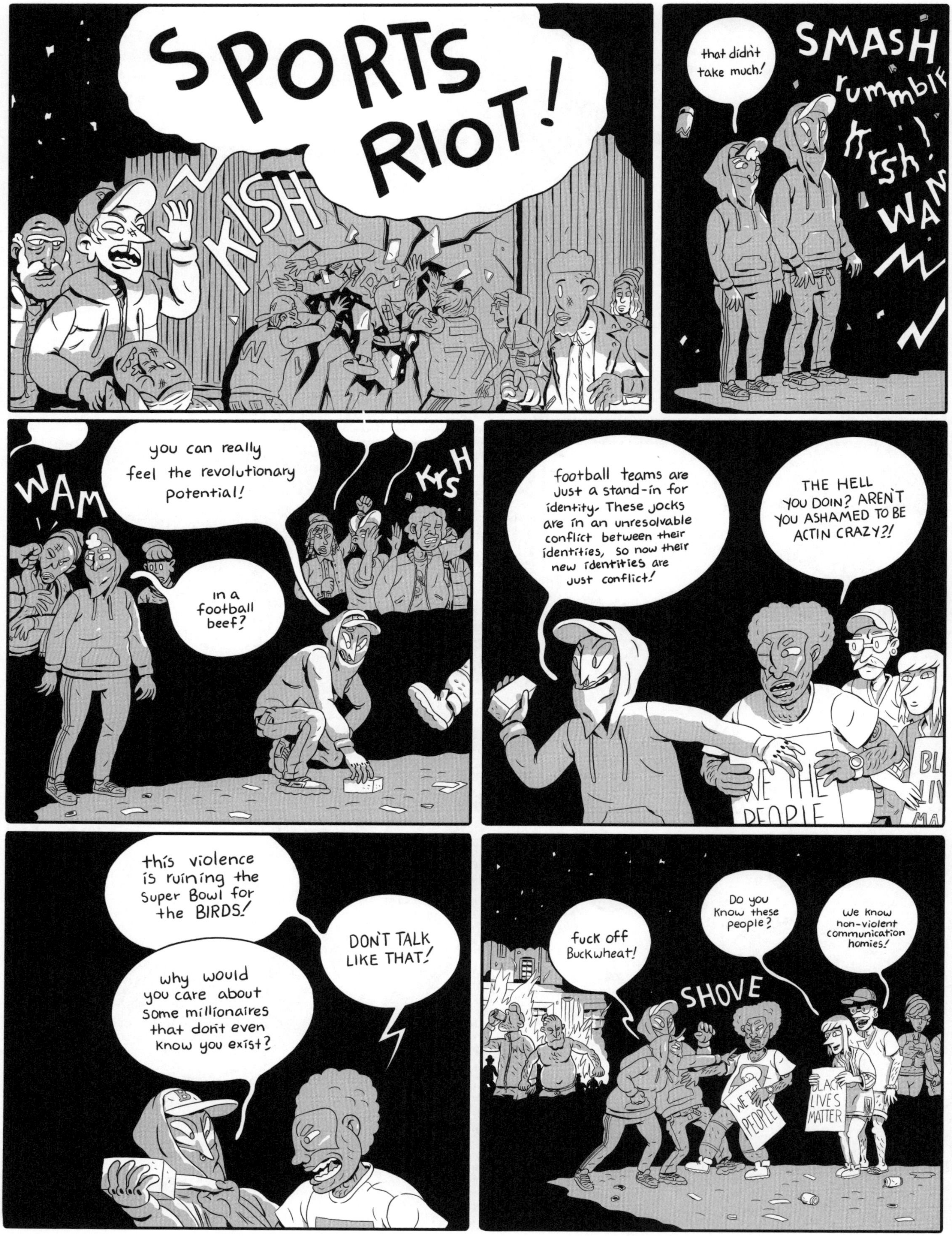
SPORTS RIOT!
KISH
that didn't take much!
SMASH
rummble
krsh!
WAM
WAM
you can really feel the revolutionary potential!
KRSH
in a football beef?
football teams are just a stand-in for identity. These jocks are in an unresolvable conflict between their identities, so now their new identities are just conflict!
THE HELL YOU DOIN? AREN'T YOU ASHAMED TO BE ACTIN CRAZY?!
WE THE PEOPLE
this violence is ruining the Super Bowl for the BIRDS!
DON'T TALK LIKE THAT!
why would you care about some millionaires that don't even know you exist?
fuck off Buckwheat!
SHOVE
Do you know these people?
We know non-violent communication homies!
WE THE PEOPLE
BLACK LIVES MATTER

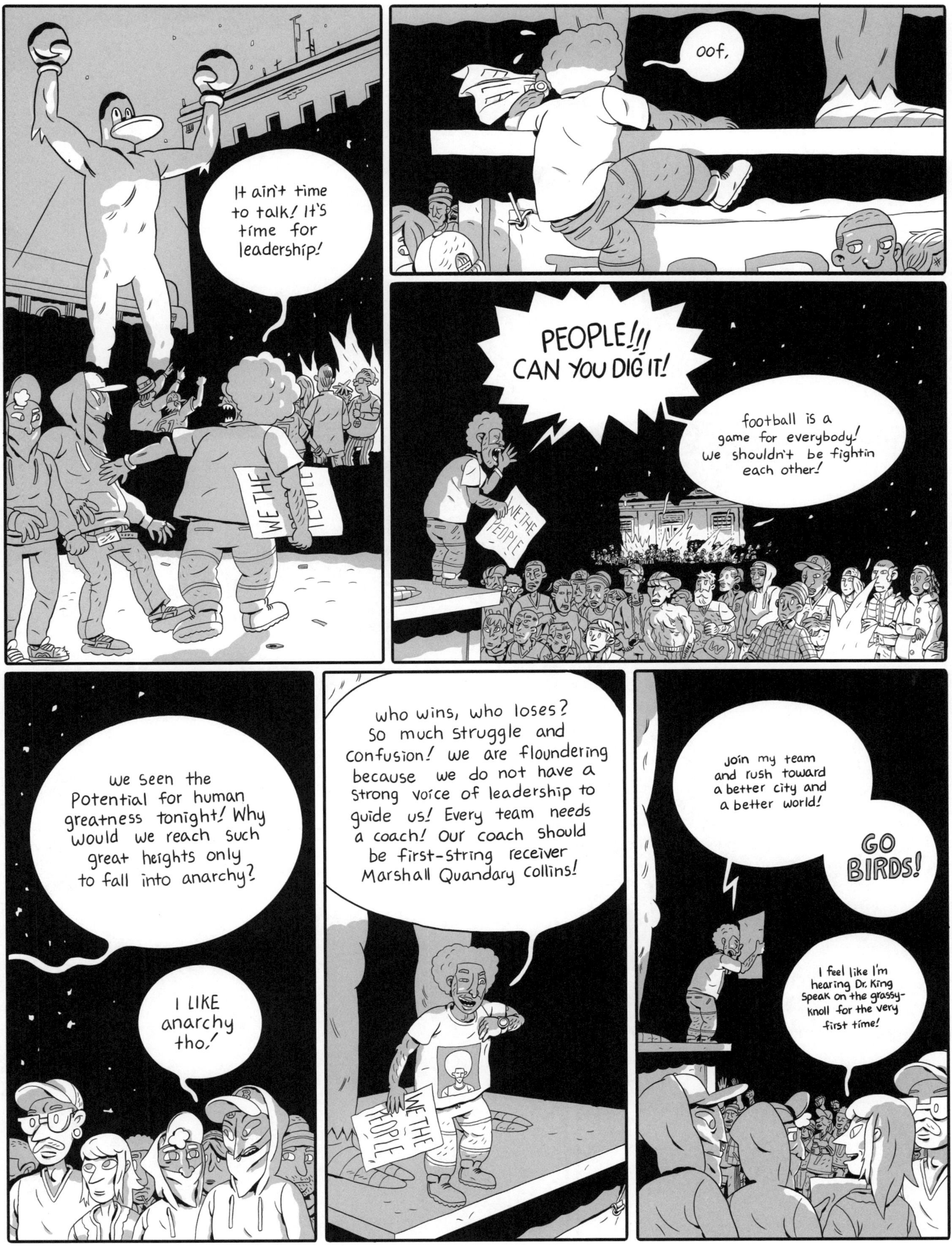
It ain't time to talk! It's time for leadership!
WE THE PEOPLE
oof,
PEOPLE!!! CAN YOU DIG IT!
football is a game for everybody! we shouldn't be fightin each other!
WE THE PEOPLE
we seen the Potential for human greatness tonight! Why would we reach such great heights only to fall into anarchy?
I LIKE anarchy tho!
who wins, who loses? So much struggle and confusion! we are floundering because we do not have a strong voice of leadership to guide us! Every team needs a coach! Our coach should be first-string receiver Marshall Quandary Collins!
WE THE PEOPLE
Join my team and rush toward a better city and a better world!
GO BIRDS!
I feel like I'm hearing Dr. King Speak on the grassy-knoll for the very first time!

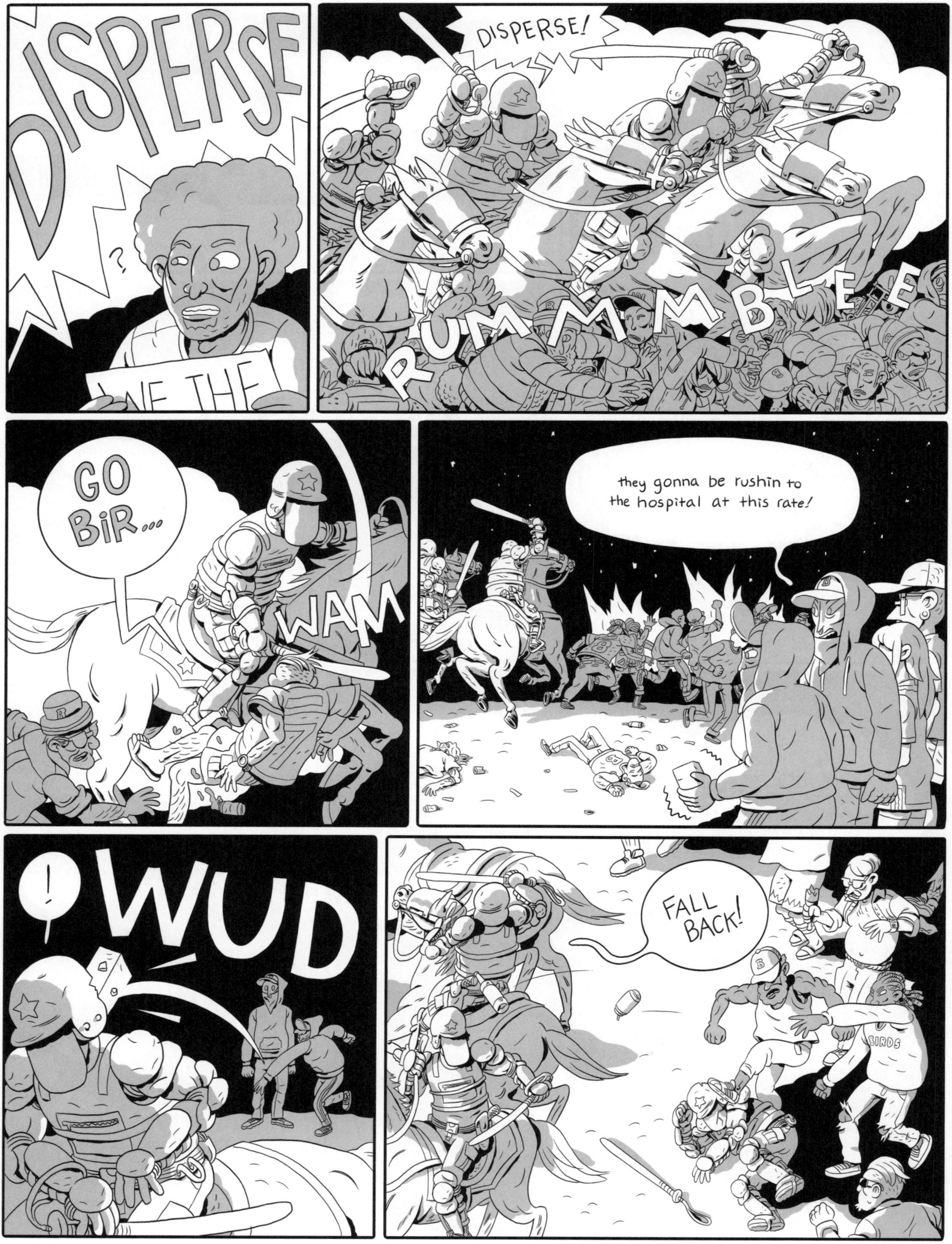
DISPERSE
?
WE THE
DISPERSE!
RUMMMBLEE
GO BiR...
WAM
they gonna be rushin to the hospital at this rate!
!
WUD
FALL BACK!
BIRDS

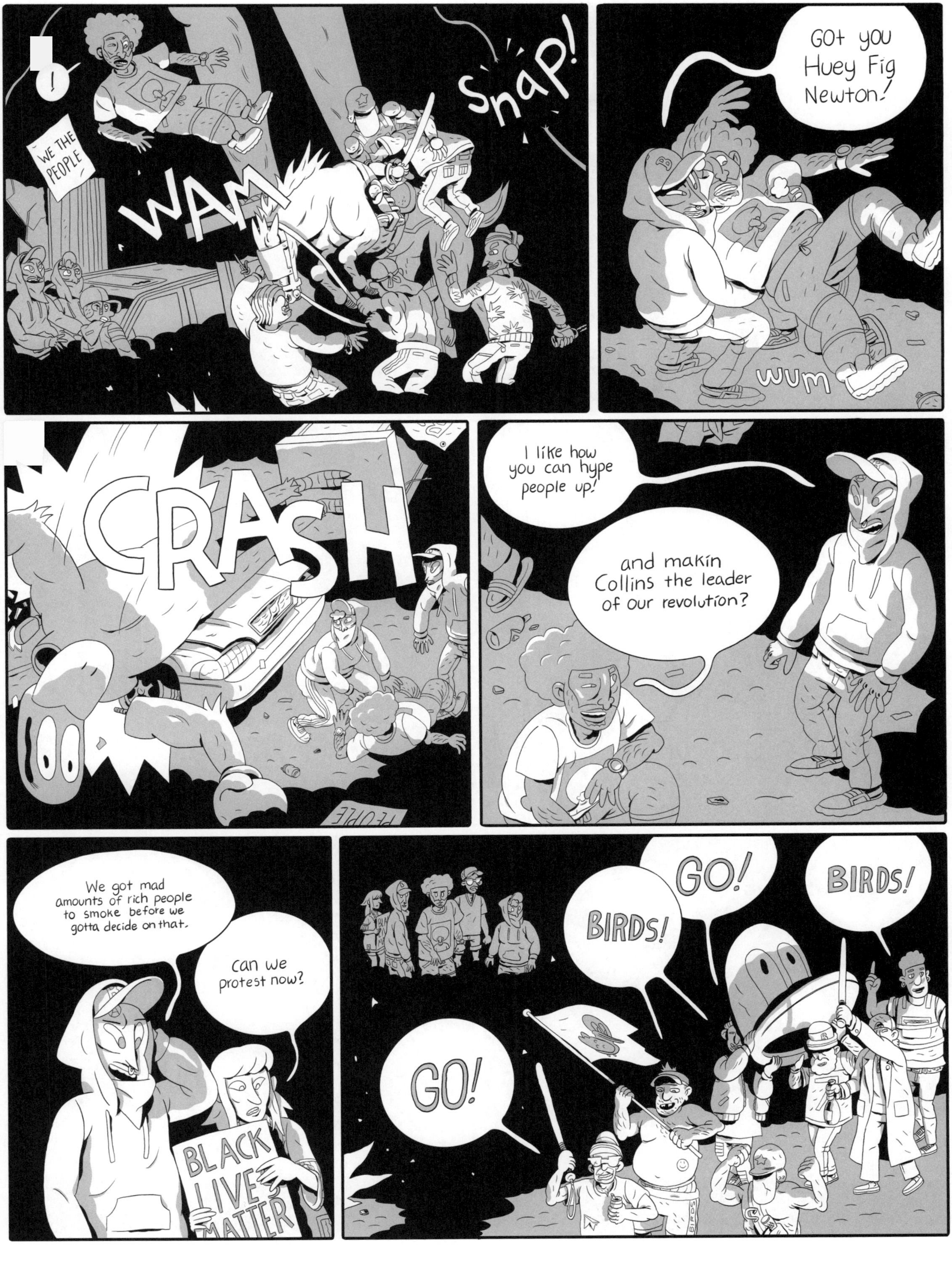
!
WE THE PEOPLE
WAM
SNAP!
GOt you Huey Fig Newton!
WUM
CRASH
I like how you can hype people up!
and makin Collins the leader of our revolution?
We got mad amounts of rich people to smoke before we gotta decide on that.
can we protest now?
BIRDS!
GO!
BIRDS!
GO!

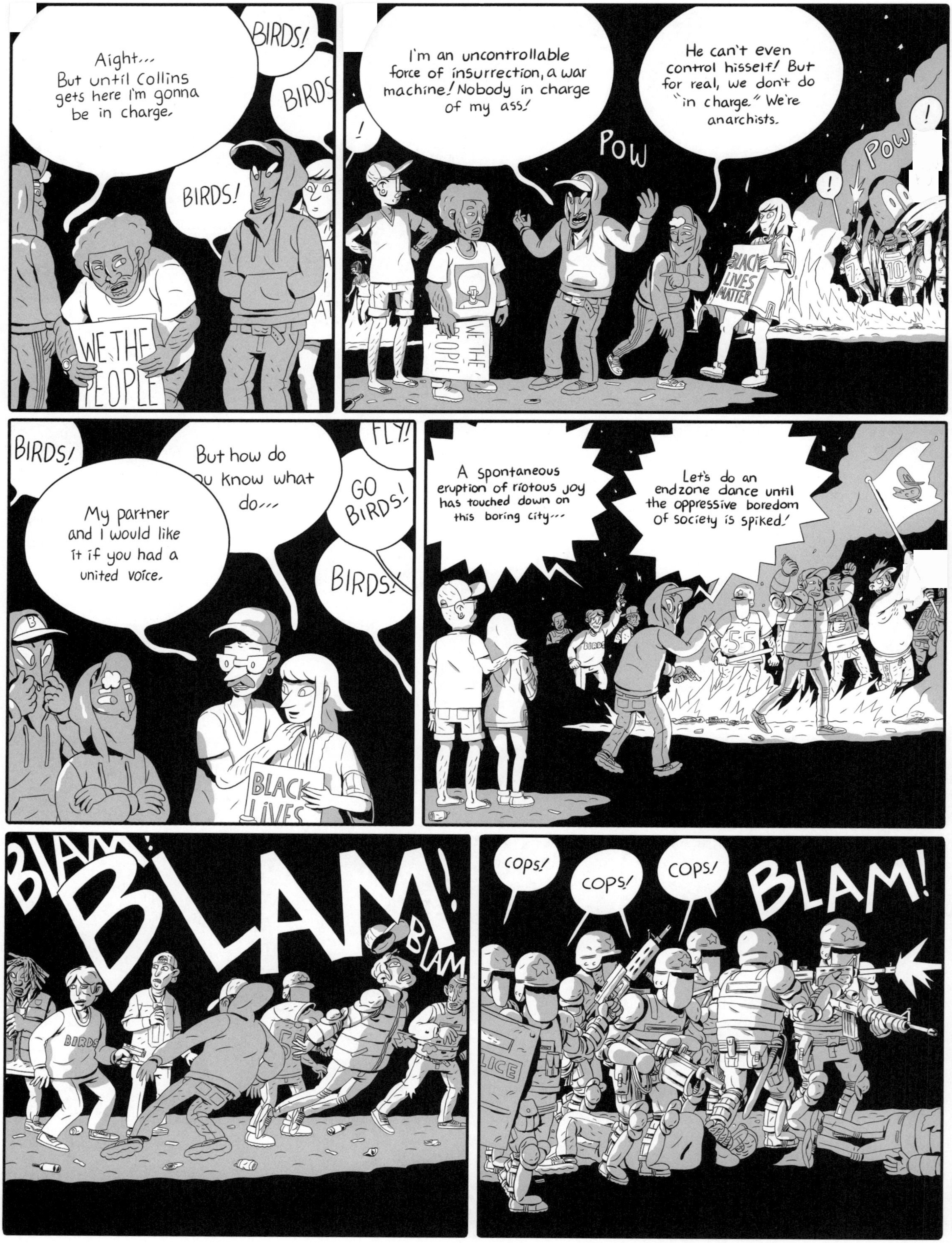
Aight...
But until Collins gets here I'm gonna be in charge.
BIRDS!
BIRDS
BIRDS!
WE THE PEOPLE
I'm an uncontrollable force of insurrection, a war machine! Nobody in charge of my ass!
!
POW
He can't even control hisself! But for real, we don't do "in charge." We're anarchists.
!
!
POW
WE THE PEOPLE
BLACK LIVES MATTER
BIRDS!
But how do you know what do...
FLY!
GO BIRDS!
My partner and I would like it if you had a united voice.
BIRDS!
BLACK LIVES
A spontaneous eruption of riotous joy has touched down on this boring city...
Let's do an endzone dance until the oppressive boredom of society is spiked!
BIRDS
55
BLAM!
BLAM!
BLAM
BLAM
BIRDS
COPS!
COPS!
COPS!
BLAM!
LICE

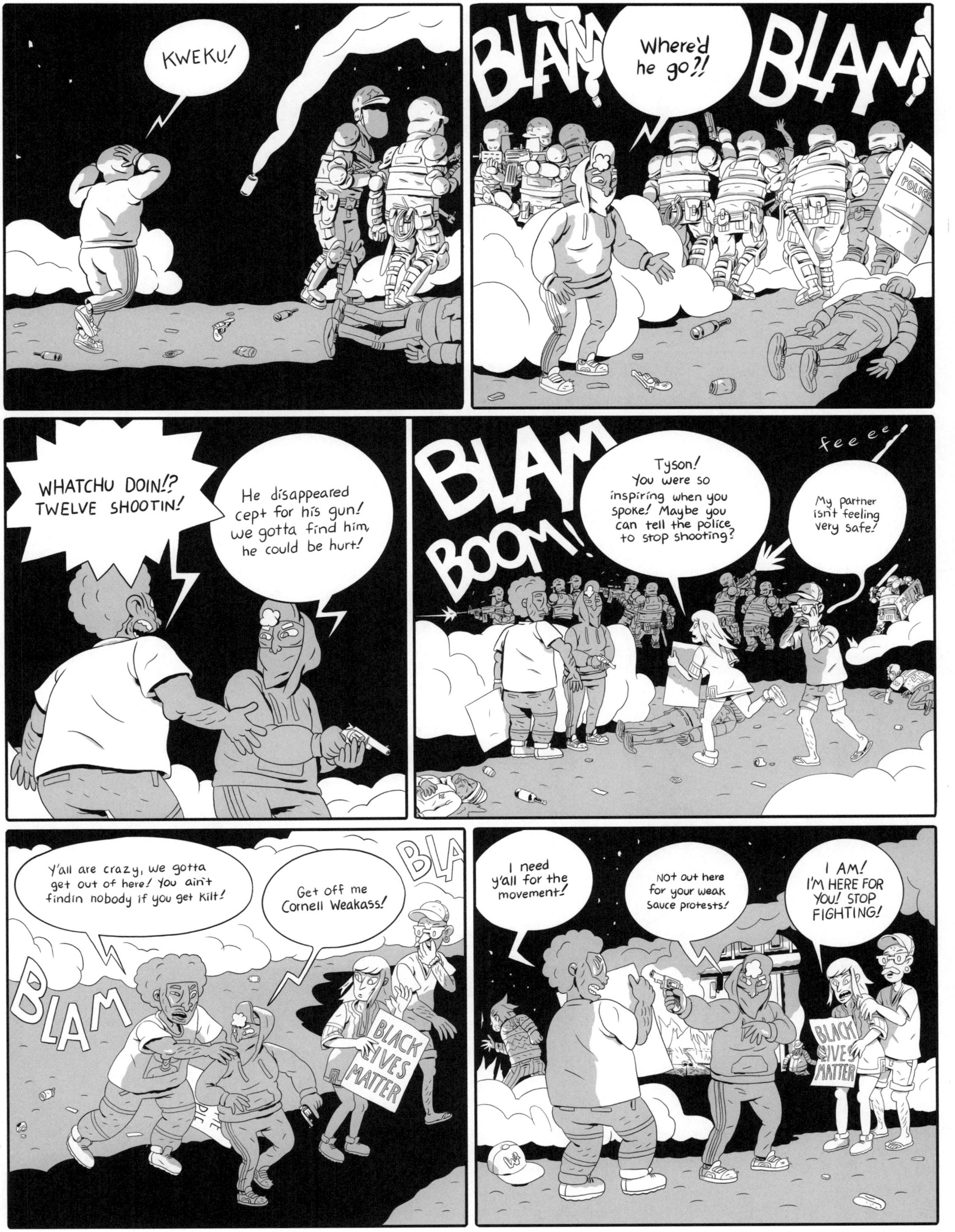
KWEKU!
BLAM
Where'd he go?!
BLAM
WHATCHU DOIN!? TWELVE SHOOTIN!
He disappeared cept for his gun! we gotta find him, he could be hurt!
BLAM
BOOM!
Tyson! You were so inspiring when you spoke! Maybe you can tell the police to stop shooting?
feeee
My partner isn't feeling very safe!
Y'all are crazy, we gotta get out of here! You ain't findin nobody if you get kilt!
Get off me Cornell Weakass!
BLA
BLAM
BLACK LIVES MATTER
I need y'all for the movement!
NOT out here for your weak sauce protests!
I AM! I'M HERE FOR YOU! STOP FIGHTING!
BLACK LIVES MATTER

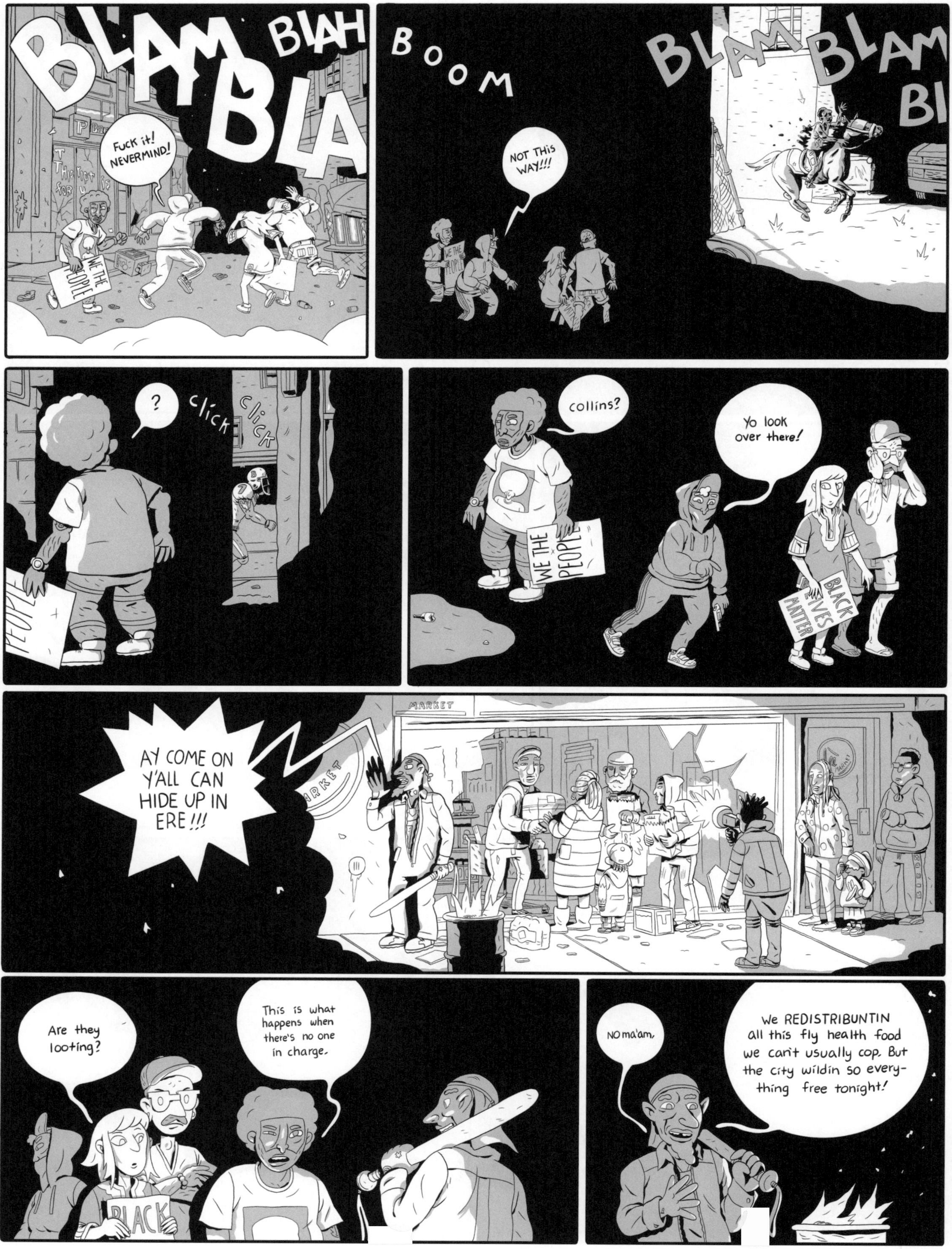
BLAM
BLAH
BLA
FUCK it! NEVERMIND!
WE THE PEOPLE
BOOM
NOT THIS WAY!!!
WE THE PEOPLE
BLAM
BLAM
?
click
click
PEOPLE
collins?
WE THE PEOPLE
Yo look over there!
BLACK LIVES MATTER
AY COME ON Y'ALL CAN HIDE UP IN ERE!!!
MARKET
MARKET
Are they looting?
This is what happens when there's no one in charge.
BLACK
NO ma'am.
We REDISTRIBUNTIN all this fly health food we can't usually cop. But the city wildin so every-thing free tonight!

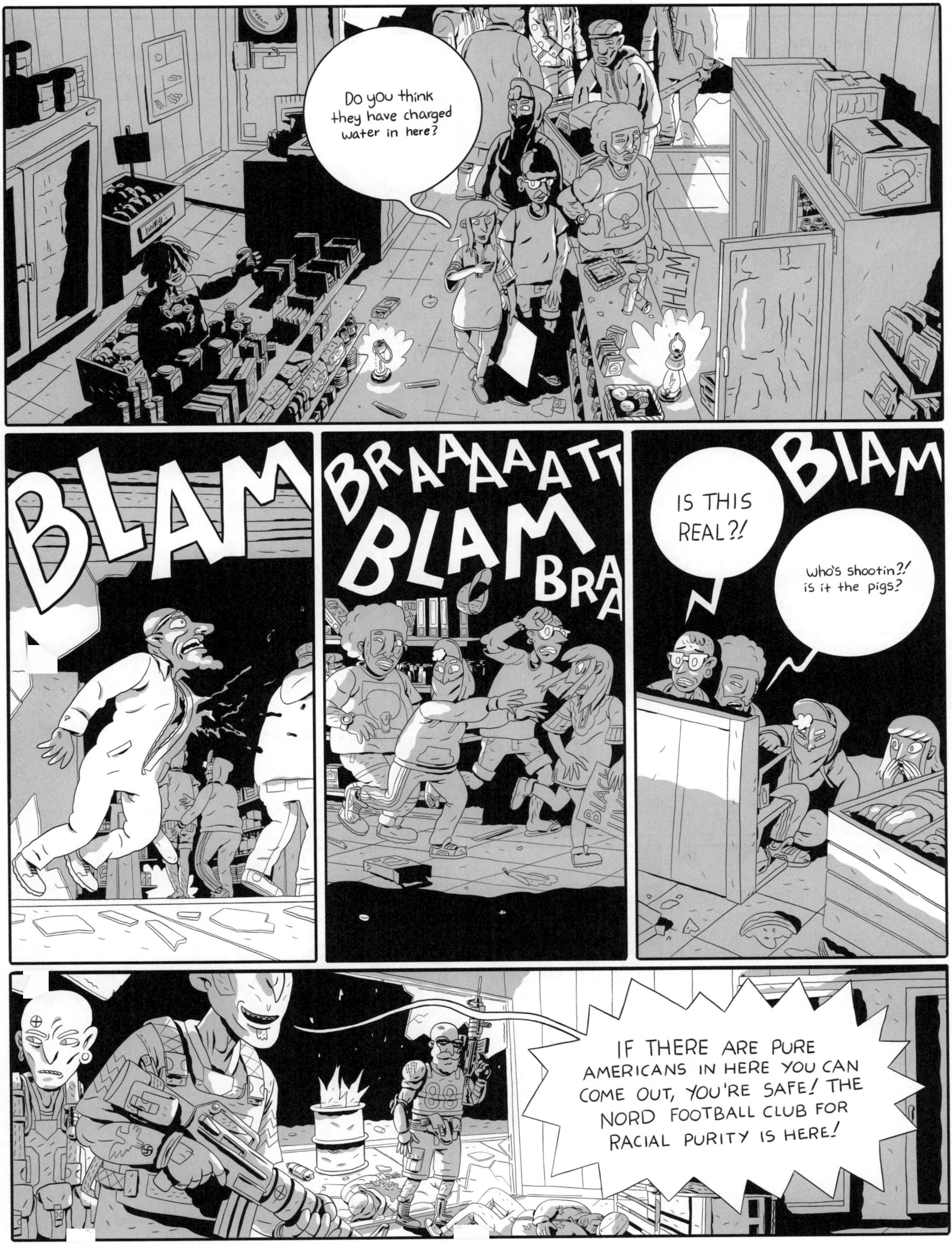
Do you think they have charged water in here?
BLAM
BRAAAAATT
BLAM
BRA
IS THIS REAL?!
BIAM
Who's shootin?! is it the pigs?
IF THERE ARE PURE AMERICANS IN HERE YOU CAN COME OUT, YOU'RE SAFE! THE NORD FOOTBALL CLUB FOR RACIAL PURITY IS HERE!

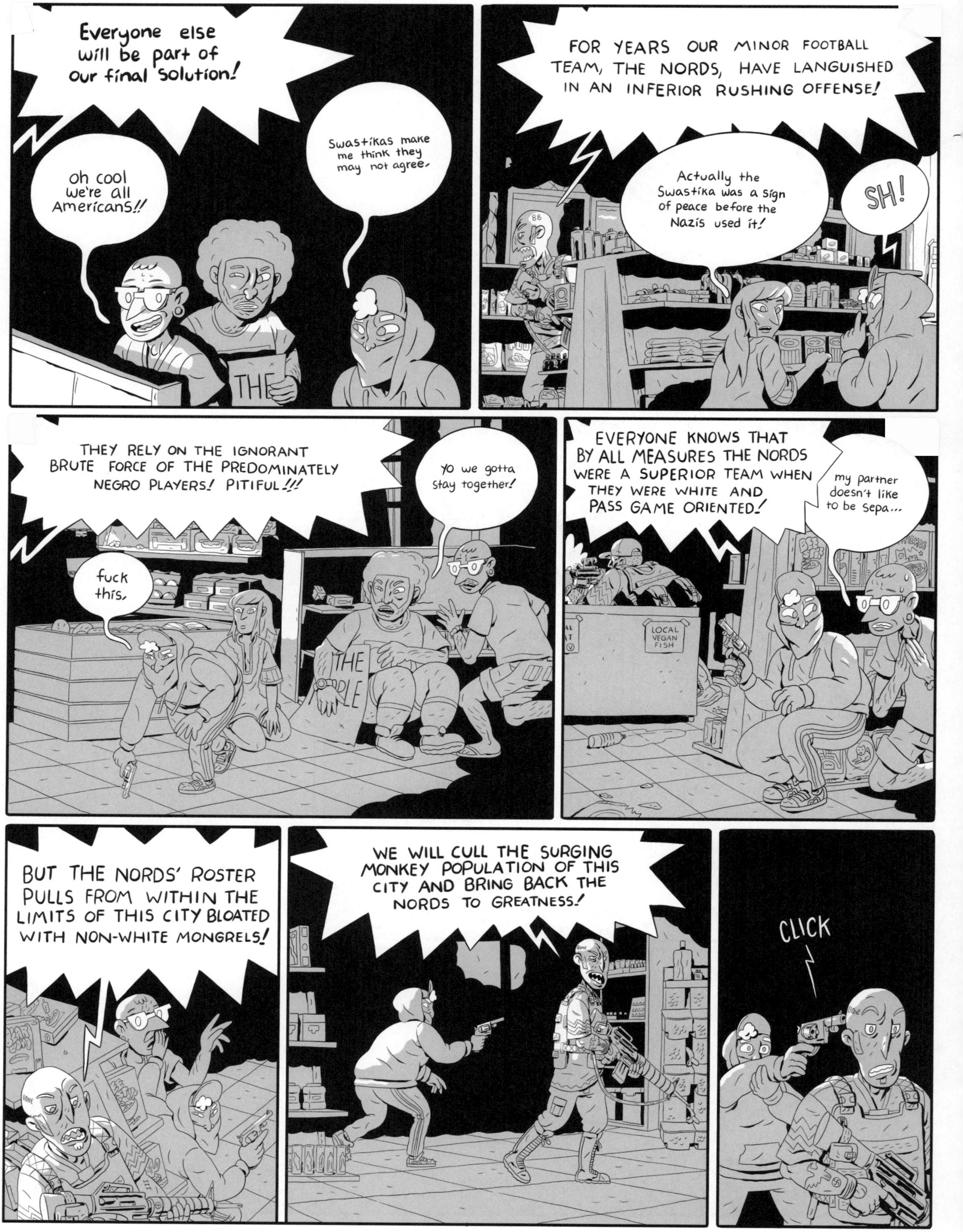
Everyone else will be part of our final solution!
Oh cool we're all Americans!!
Swastikas make me think they may not agree.
THE
FOR YEARS OUR MINOR FOOTBALL TEAM, THE NORDS, HAVE LANGUISHED IN AN INFERIOR RUSHING OFFENSE!
88
Actually the Swastika was a sign of peace before the Nazis used it!
SH!
THEY RELY ON THE IGNORANT BRUTE FORCE OF THE PREDOMINATELY NEGRO PLAYERS! PITIFUL!!!
Yo we gotta stay together!
fuck this.
EVERYONE KNOWS THAT BY ALL MEASURES THE NORDS WERE A SUPERIOR TEAM WHEN THEY WERE WHITE AND PASS GAME ORIENTED!
my partner doesn't like to be sepa...
LOCAL VEGAN FISH
BUT THE NORDS' ROSTER PULLS FROM WITHIN THE LIMITS OF THIS CITY BLOATED WITH NON-WHITE MONGRELS!
WE WILL CULL THE SURGING MONKEY POPULATION OF THIS CITY AND BRING BACK THE NORDS TO GREATNESS!
CLICK

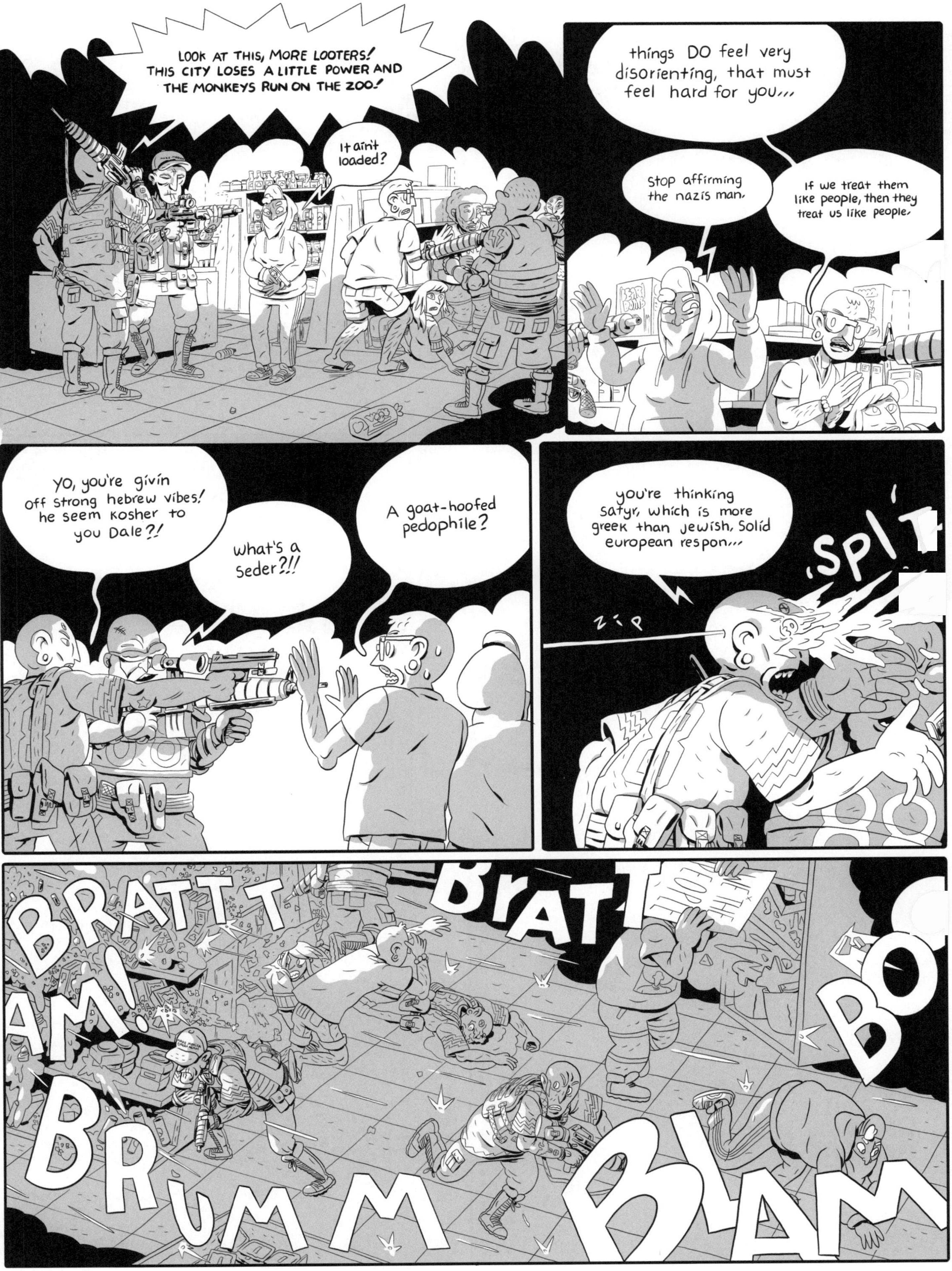
LOOK AT THIS, MORE LOOTERS! THIS CITY LOSES A LITTLE POWER AND THE MONKEYS RUN ON THE ZOO!
It ain't loaded?
things DO feel very disorienting, that must feel hard for you...
Stop affirming the nazis man.
If we treat them like people, then they treat us like people.
YO, you're givin off strong hebrew vibes! he seem kosher to you Dale?!
what's a seder?!!
A goat-hoofed pedophile?
you're thinking satyr, which is more greek than jewish. Solid european respon...
zip
SPIT
BRATT T
BRATT
AM!
BO
BRUMM M
BLAM

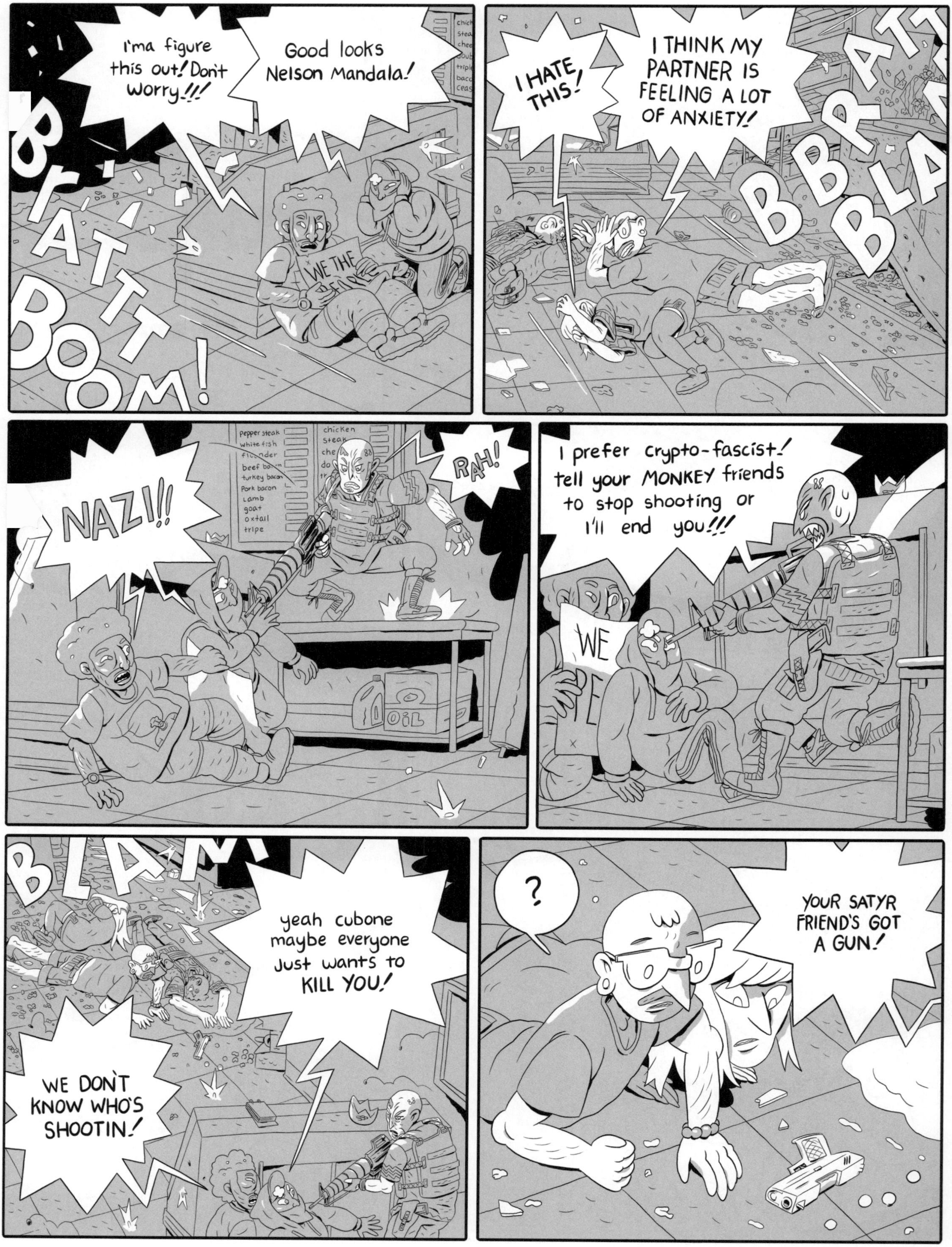
I'ma figure this out! Don't worry!!!
Good looks Nelson Mandala!
WE THE
BRATTT BOOM!
I HATE THIS!
I THINK MY PARTNER IS FEELING A LOT OF ANXIETY!
BBRATT
BLA
pepper steak
white fish
flounder
beef bacon
turkey bacon
pork bacon
lamb
goat
oxtail
tripe
chicken
steak
NAZI!!
RAH!
OIL
I prefer crypto-fascist! tell your MONKEY friends to stop shooting or I'll end you!!!
WE
BLAM
yeah cubone maybe everyone just wants to KILL YOU!
WE DON'T KNOW WHO'S SHOOTIN!
?
YOUR SATYR FRIEND'S GOT A GUN!

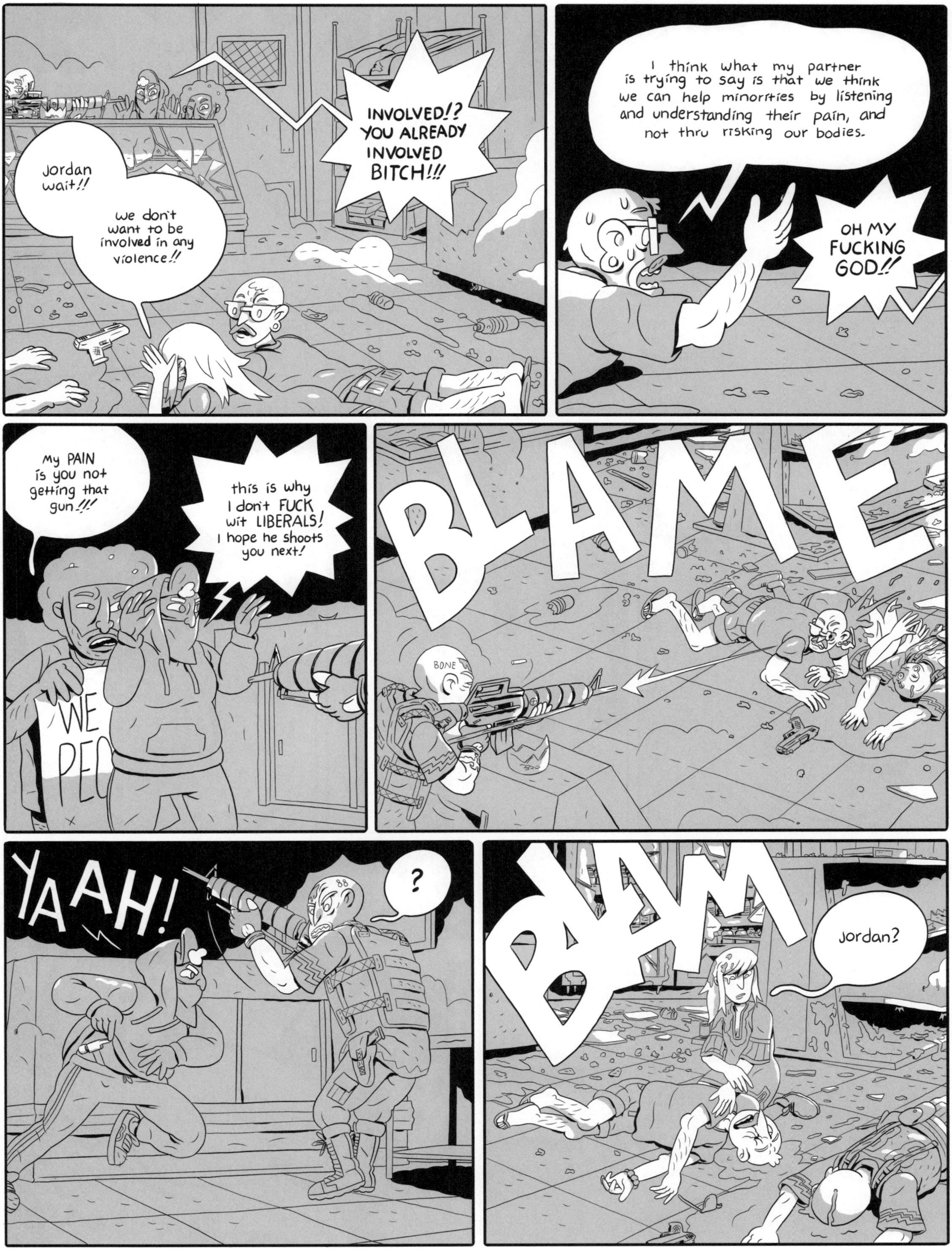

Jordan wait!!
we don't want to be involved in any violence!!
INVOLVED!? YOU ALREADY INVOLVED BITCH!!!
I think what my partner is trying to say is that we think we can help minorities by listening and understanding their pain, and not thru risking our bodies.
OH MY FUCKING GOD!!
My PAIN is you not getting that gun!!!
this is why I don't FUCK wit LIBERALS! I hope he shoots you next!
WE PEO
BLAME
BONE
YAAH!
88
?
BLAM
Jordan?

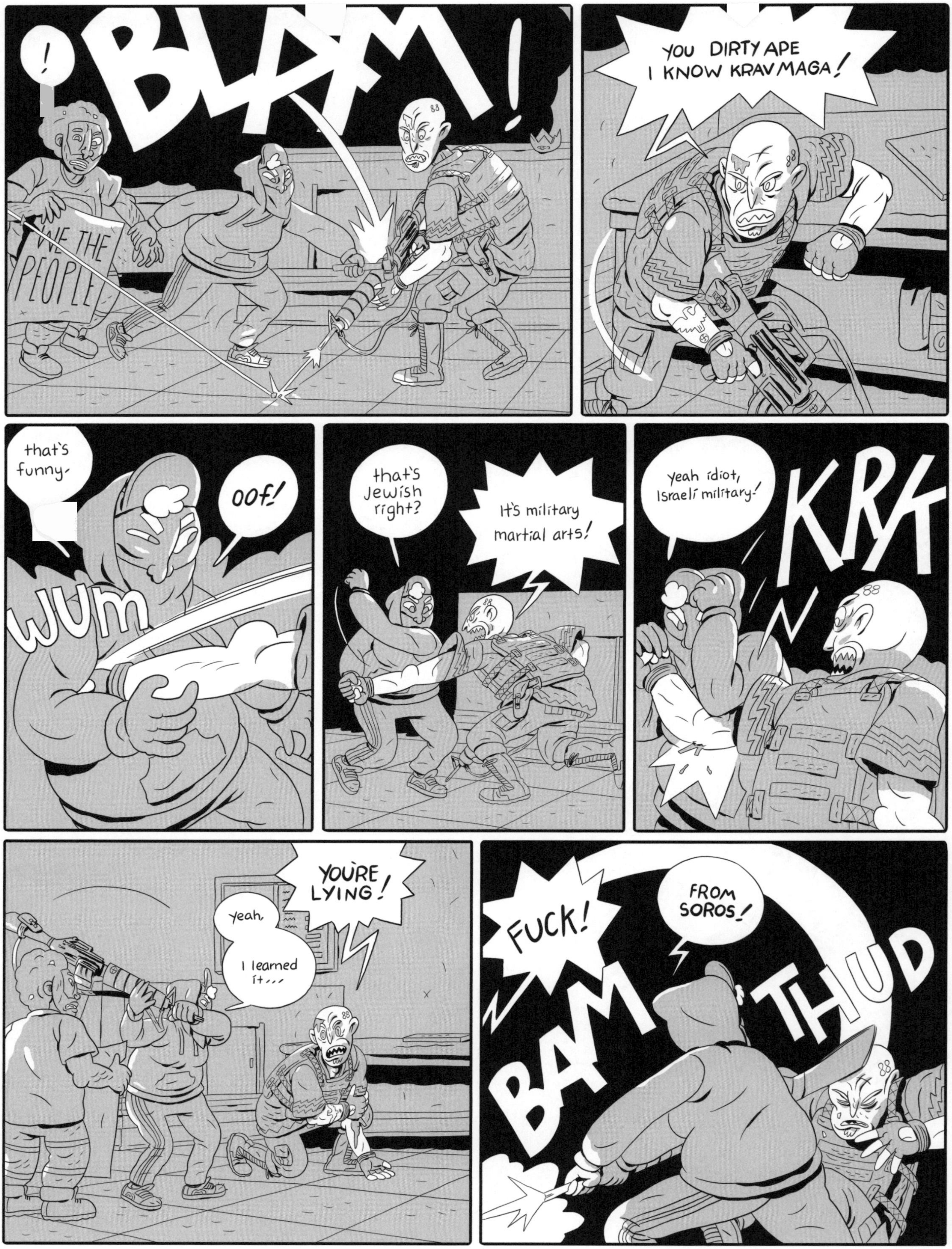
!
BLAM!
WE THE PEOPLE
YOU DIRTY APE I KNOW KRAV MAGA!
that's funny.
WUM
oof!
that's Jewish right?
It's military martial arts!
yeah idiot, Israeli military!
KRK
YOU'RE LYING!
yeah,
I learned it...
FUCK!
FROM SOROS!
BAM
THUD

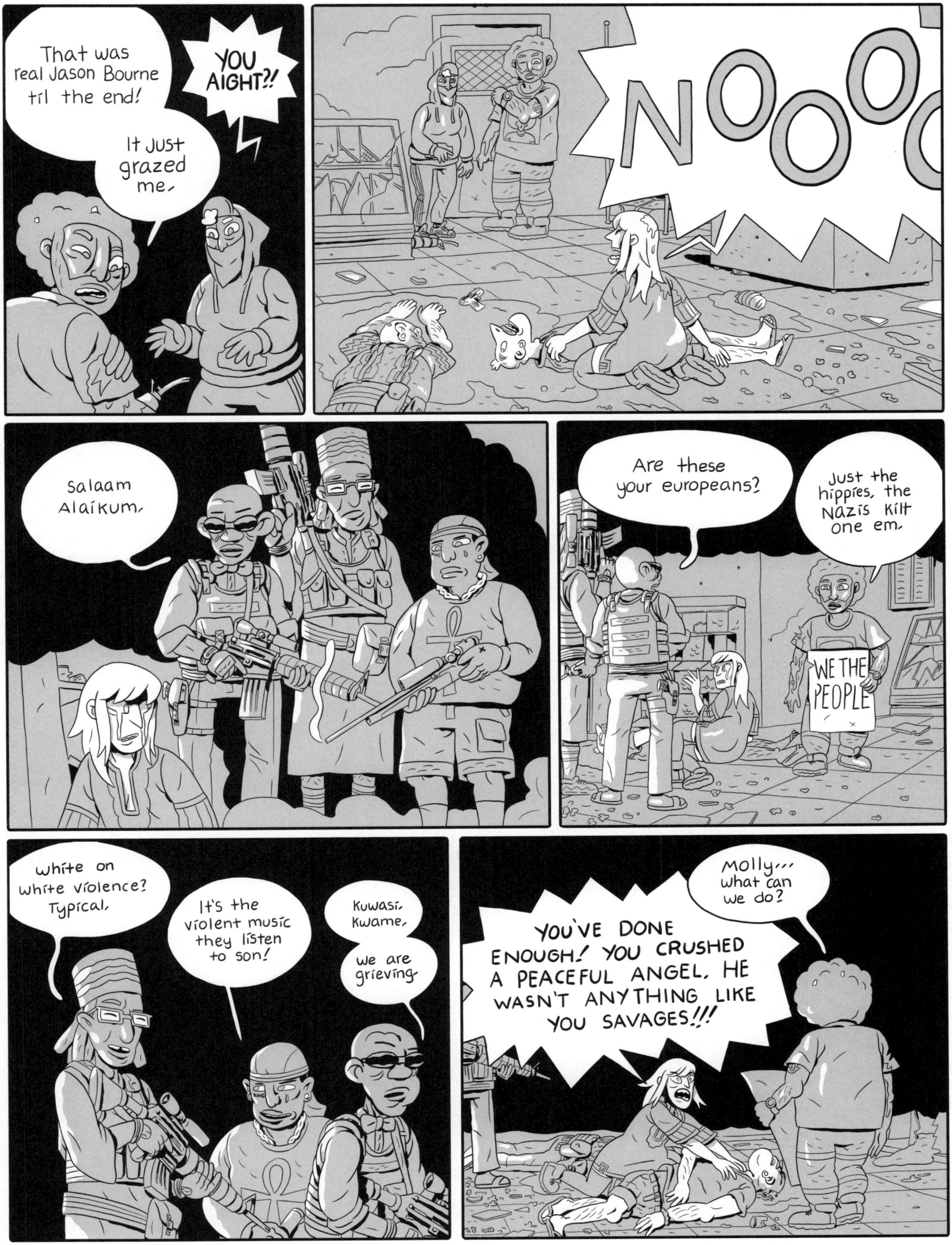
That was real Jason Bourne til the end!
YOU AIGHT?!
It just grazed me.
NOOOO
Salaam Alaikum.
Are these your europeans?
Just the hippies, the Nazis kilt one em.
WE THE PEOPLE
White on white violence? Typical.
It's the violent music they listen to son!
Kuwasi. Kwame,
we are grieving.
Molly... what can we do?
YOU'VE DONE ENOUGH! YOU CRUSHED A PEACEFUL ANGEL. HE WASN'T ANYTHING LIKE YOU SAVAGES!!!

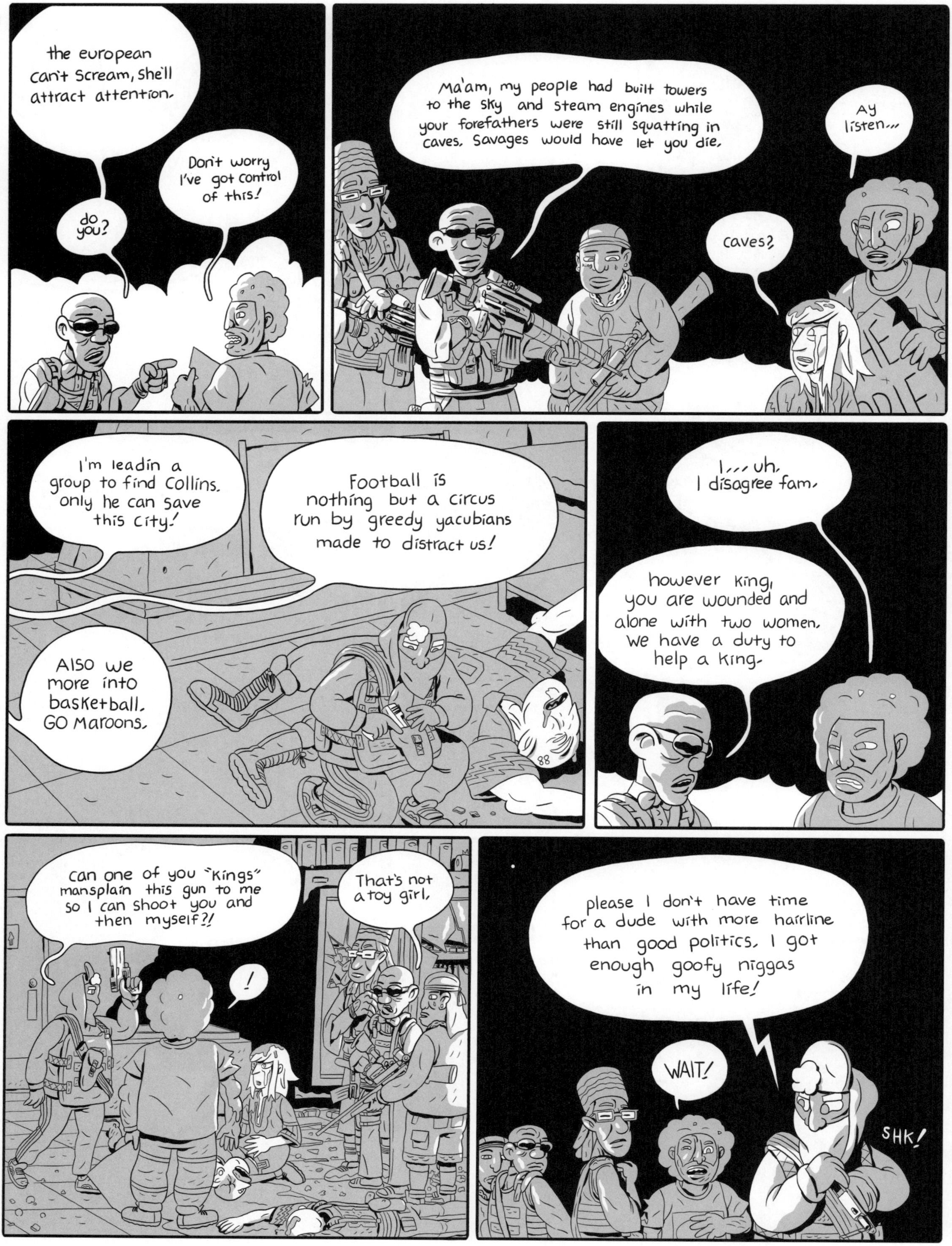
the european can't Scream, she'll attract attention.
do you?
Don't worry I've got control of this!
Ma'am, my people had built towers to the sky and steam engines while your forefathers were still squatting in caves. Savages would have let you die.
Ay listen...
caves?
I'm leadin a group to find Collins. only he can save this city!
Football is nothing but a circus run by greedy yacubians made to distract us!
Also we more into basketball. GO Maroons.
I... uh. I disagree fam.
however King, you are wounded and alone with two women. We have a duty to help a King.
can one of you "Kings" mansplain this gun to me so I can shoot you and then myself?!
That's not a toy girl.
!
please I don't have time for a dude with more hairline than good politics. I got enough goofy niggas in my life!
WAIT!
SHK!

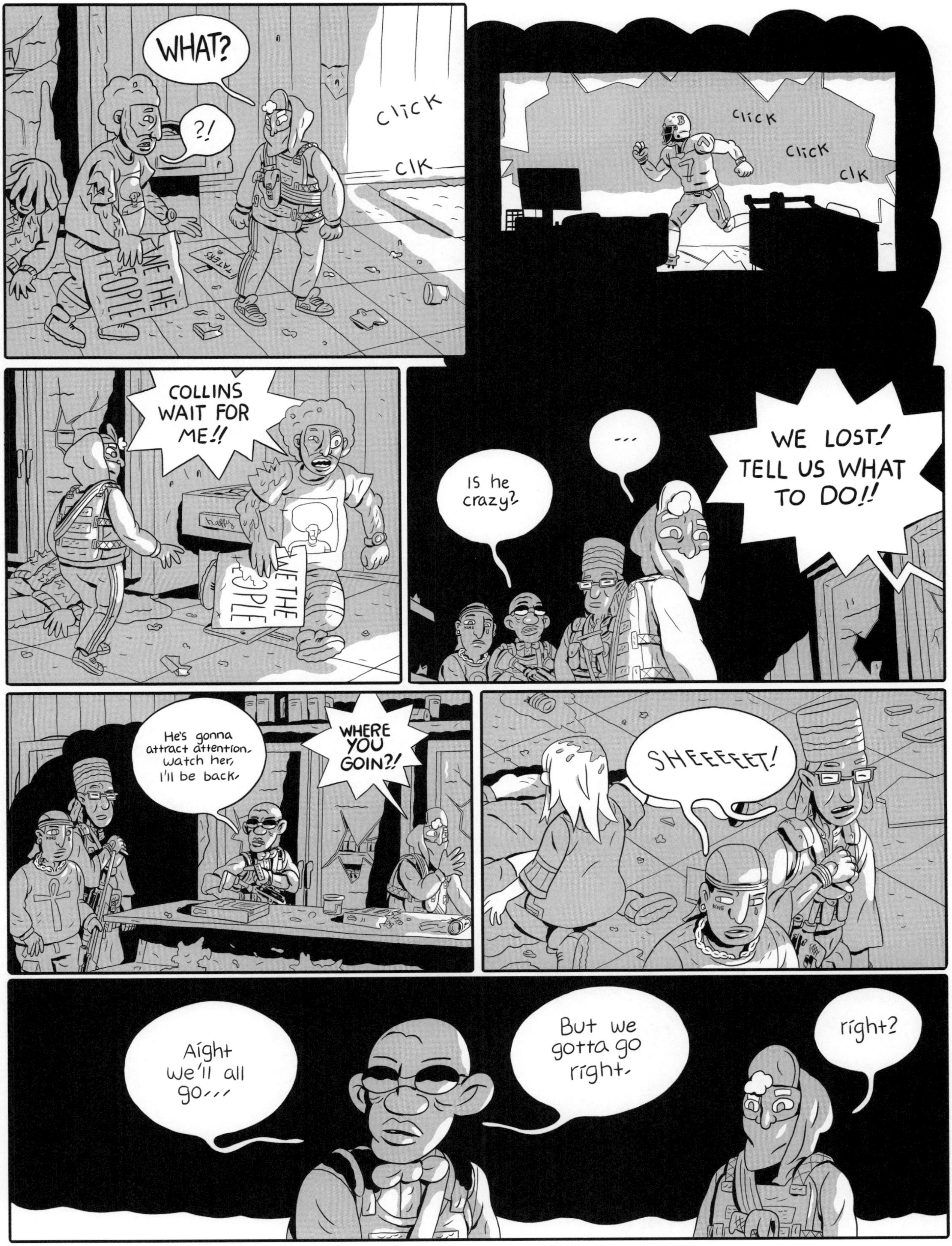
WHAT?
?!
CLICK
CLK
CLICK
CLICK
CLK
WE THE PEOPLE
COLLINS WAIT FOR ME!!
WE THE PEOPLE
Is he crazy?
...
WE LOST! TELL US WHAT TO DO!!
He's gonna attract attention. Watch her, I'll be back.
WHERE YOU GOIN?!
SHEEEEEET!
Aight we'll all go...
But we gotta go right.
right?

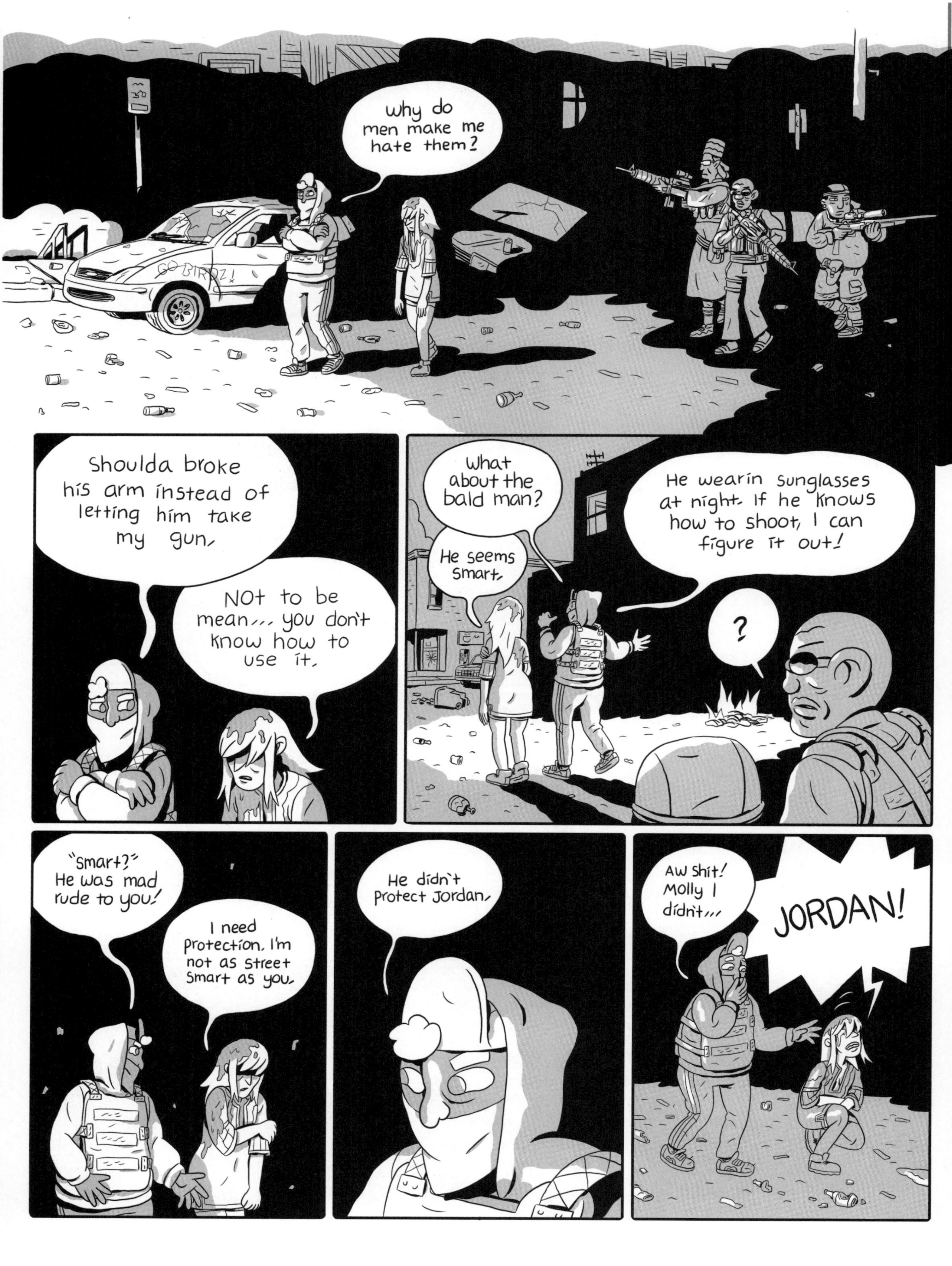

why do men make me hate them?
Shoulda broke his arm instead of letting him take my gun,
NOt to be mean,,, you don't know how to use it,
What about the bald man?
He seems smart,
He wearin sunglasses at night. If he knows how to shoot, I can figure it out!
?
"smart?" He was mad rude to you!
I need protection. I'm not as street smart as you,
He didn't protect Jordan,
Aw Shit! Molly I didn't,,,
JORDAN!

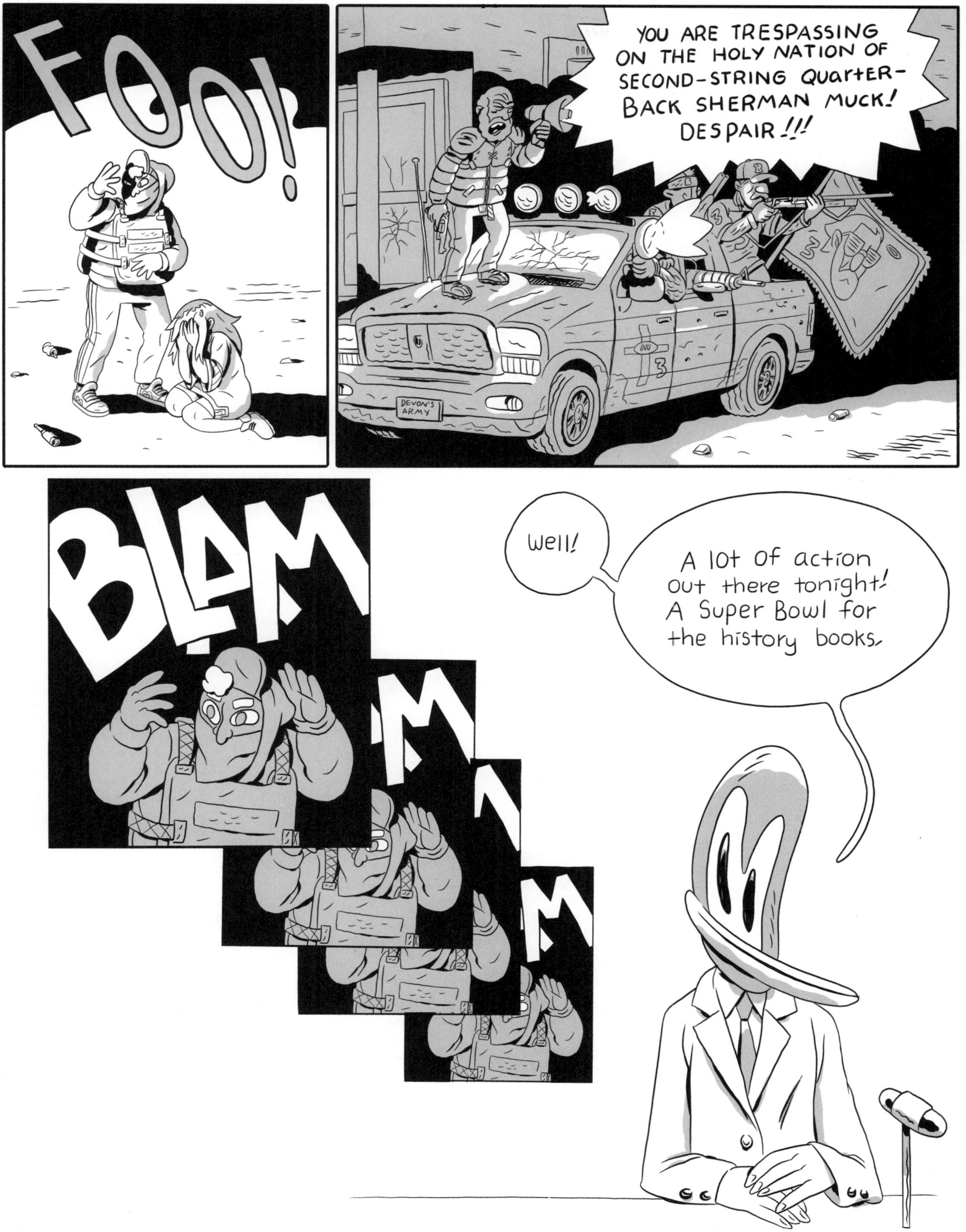

FOOM!
YOU ARE TRESPASSING ON THE HOLY NATION OF SECOND-STRING QuarterBACK SHERMAN MUCK! DESPAIR!!!
DEVON'S ARMY
BLAM
Well!
A lot of action out there tonight! A Super Bowl for the history books.

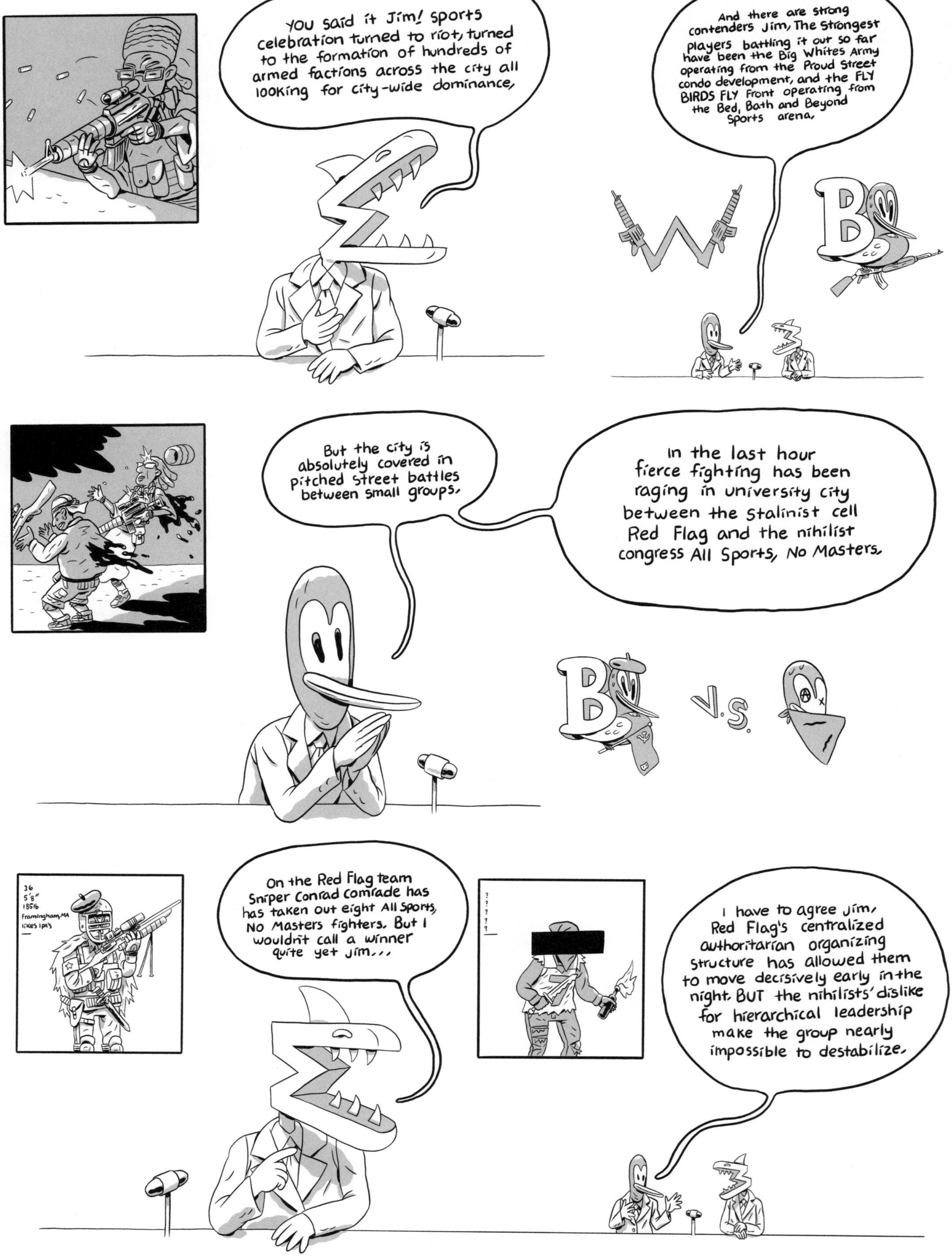

YOU said it Jim! sports celebration turned to riot, turned to the formation of hundreds of armed factions across the city all looking for city-wide dominance,
And there are strong contenders Jim, The Strongest players battling it out so far have been the Big Whites Army operating from the Proud Street condo development, and the FLY BIRDS FLY Front operating from the Bed, Bath and Beyond Sports arena,
W
B
But the city is absolutely covered in pitched street battles between small groups,
In the last hour fierce fighting has been raging in university city between the Stalinist cell Red Flag and the nihilist congress All Sports, No Masters,
B
V.S.
36
5'8"
185lb
Framingham, MA
likes IPA's
On the Red Flag team Sniper Conrad Comrade has has taken out eight All Sports, No Masters fighters. But I wouldn't call a winner quite yet Jim...
?
?
?
?
I have to agree Jim, Red Flag's centralized authoritarian organizing structure has allowed them to move decisively early in the night. BUT the nihilists' dislike for hierarchical leadership make the group nearly impossible to destabilize,

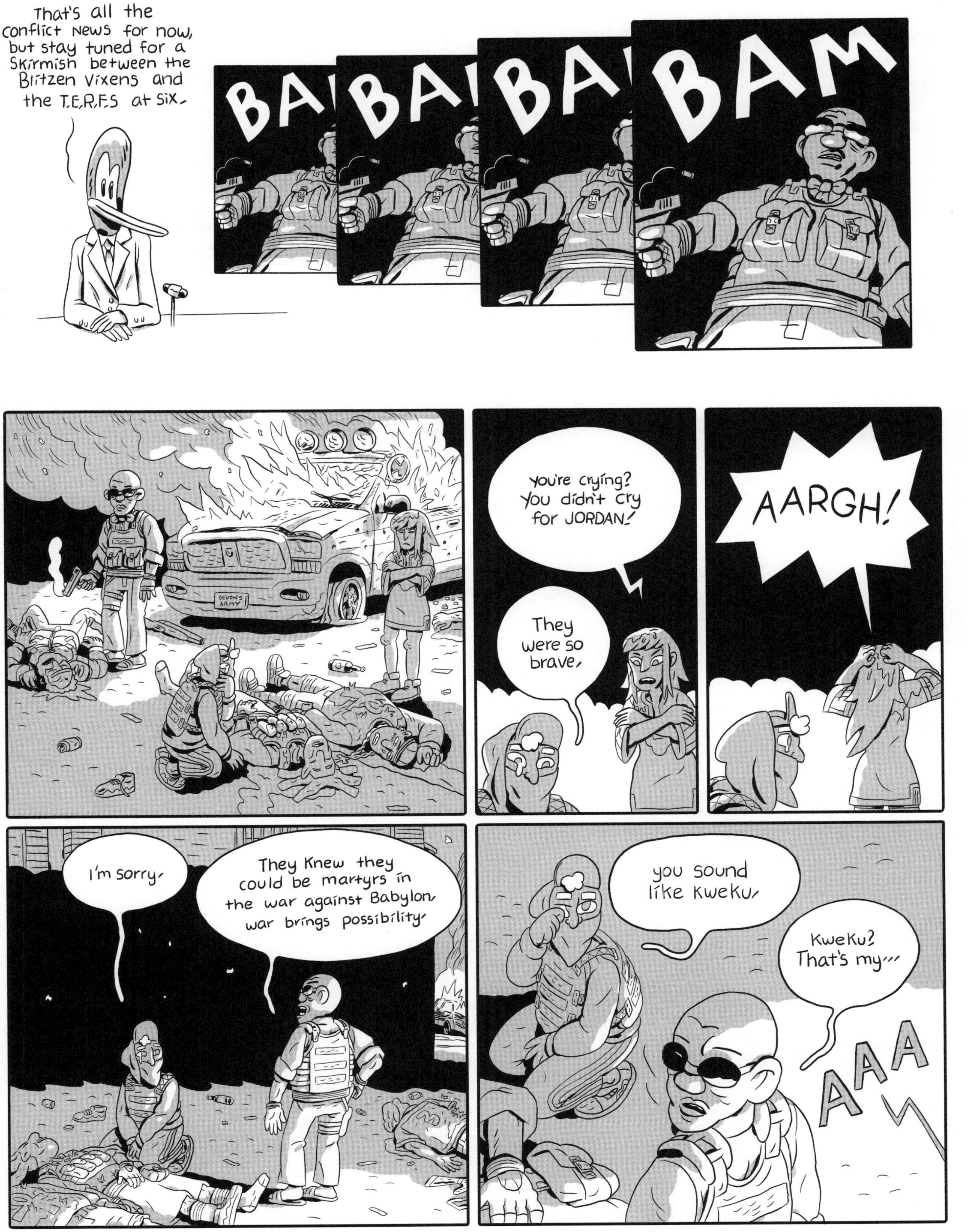
That's all the conflict news for now, but stay tuned for a skirmish between the Blitzen Vixens and the T.E.R.F.S at six.
BA
BA
BA
BAM
DEVON'S ARMY
You're crying? You didn't cry for JORDAN.
They were so brave.
AARGH!
I'm sorry.
They knew they could be martyrs in the war against Babylon. War brings possibility.
You sound like Kweku.
Kweku? That's my...
AAA

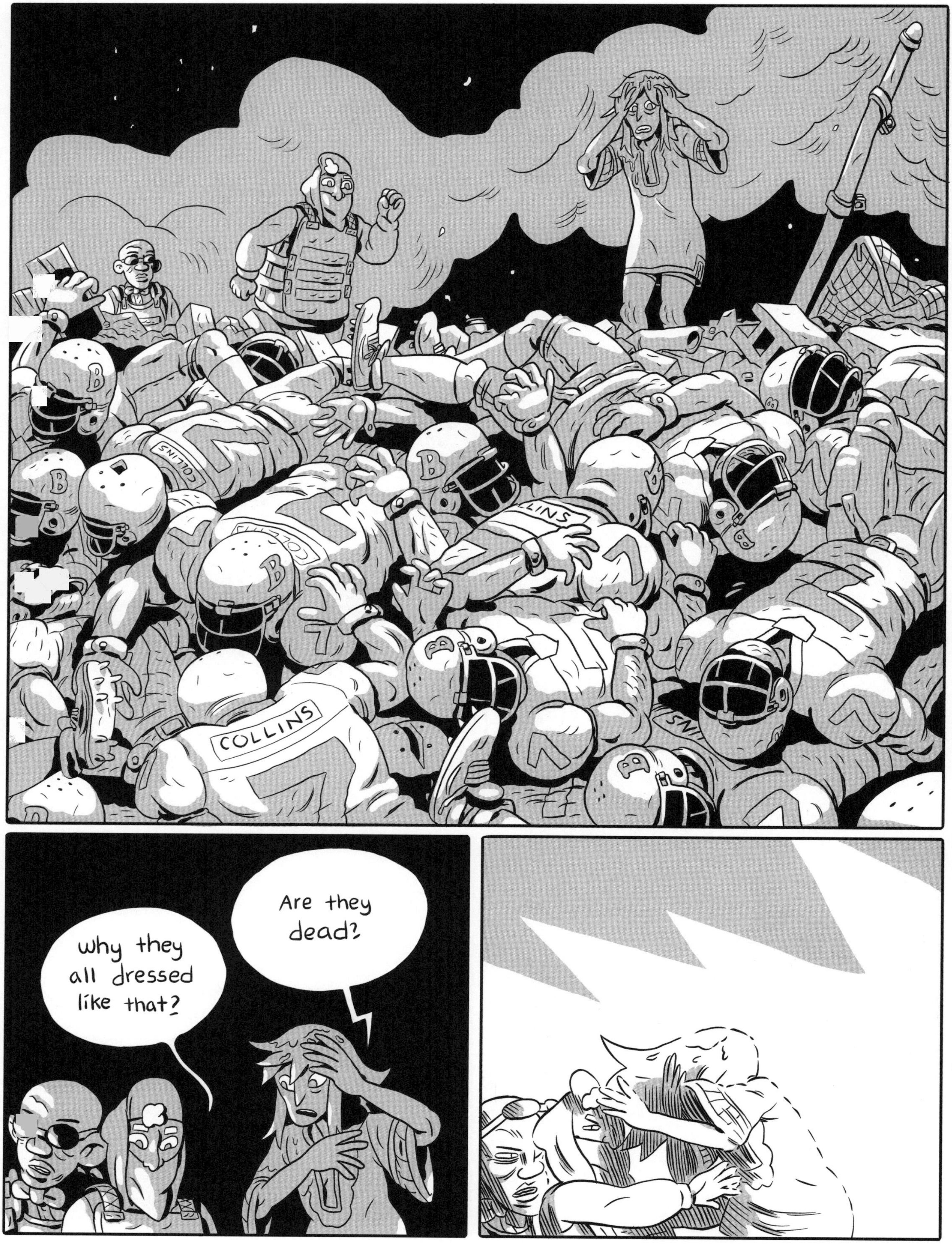
COLLINS
COLLINS
Why they all dressed like that?
Are they dead?

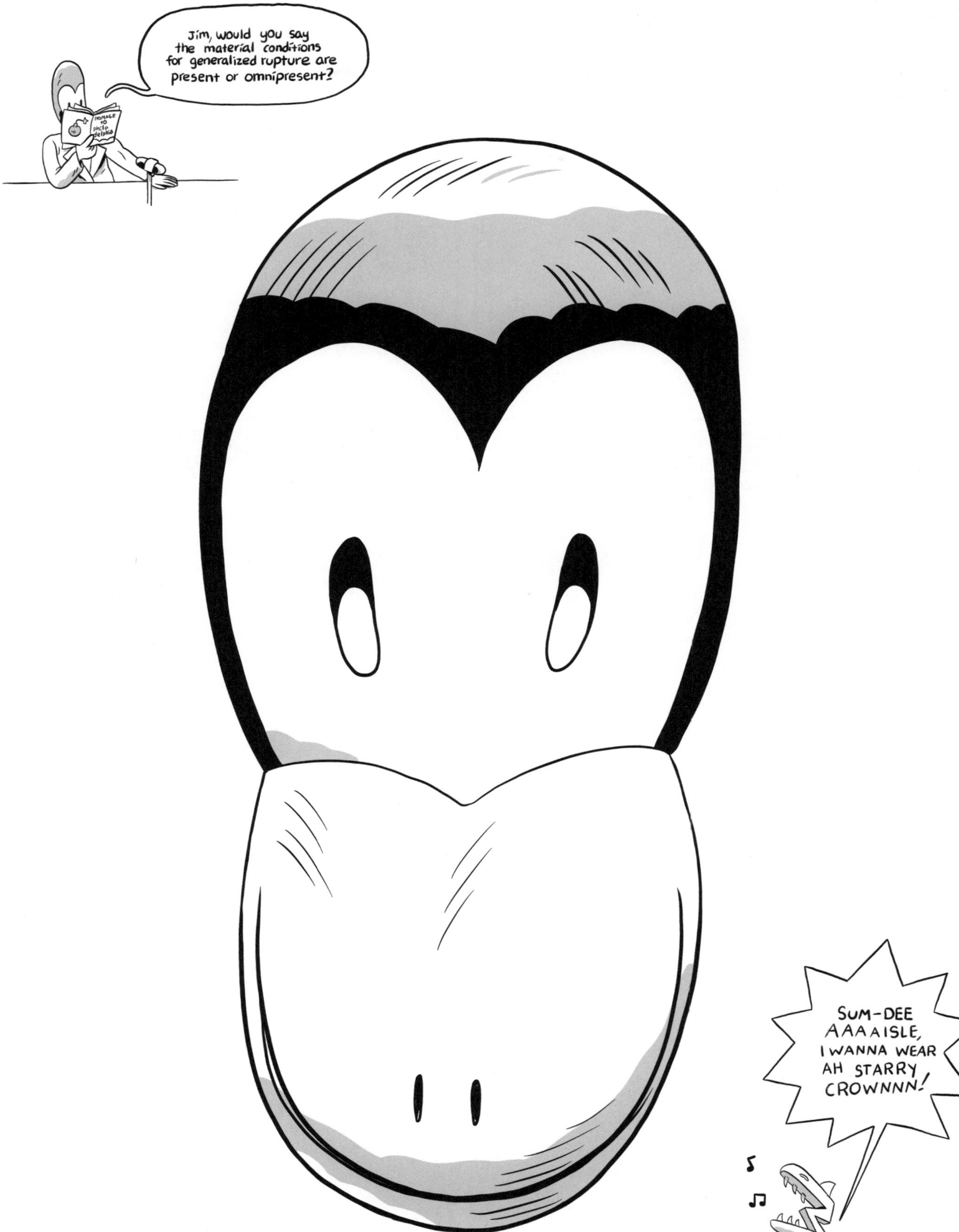
Jim, would you say the material conditions for generalized rupture are present or omnipresent?
HOMAGE TO philadelphia
SUM-DEE AAAAISLE, I WANNA WEAR AH STARRY CROWNNN!

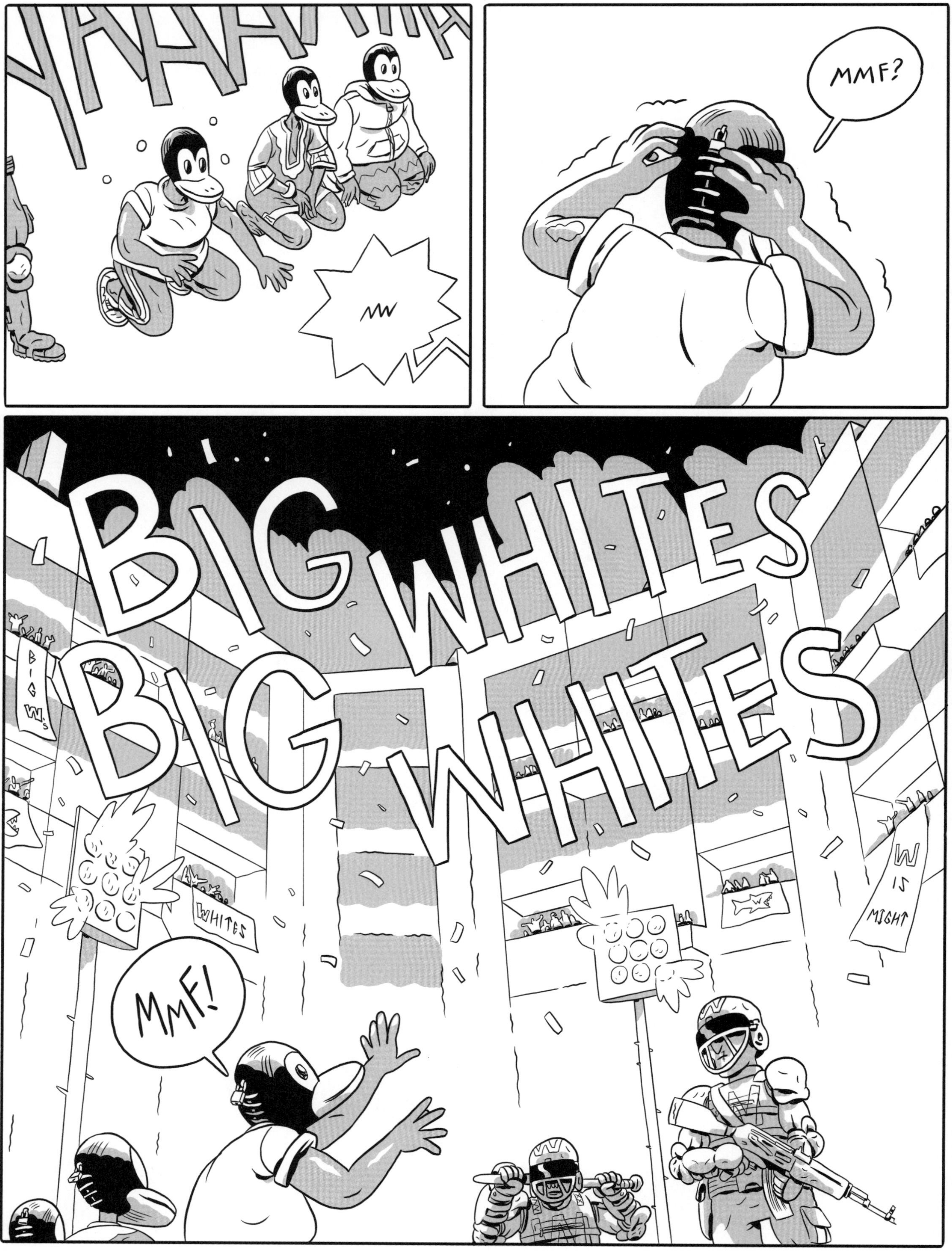
MMF?
BIG WHITES
BIG WHITES
WHITES
W IS MIGHT
MMF!

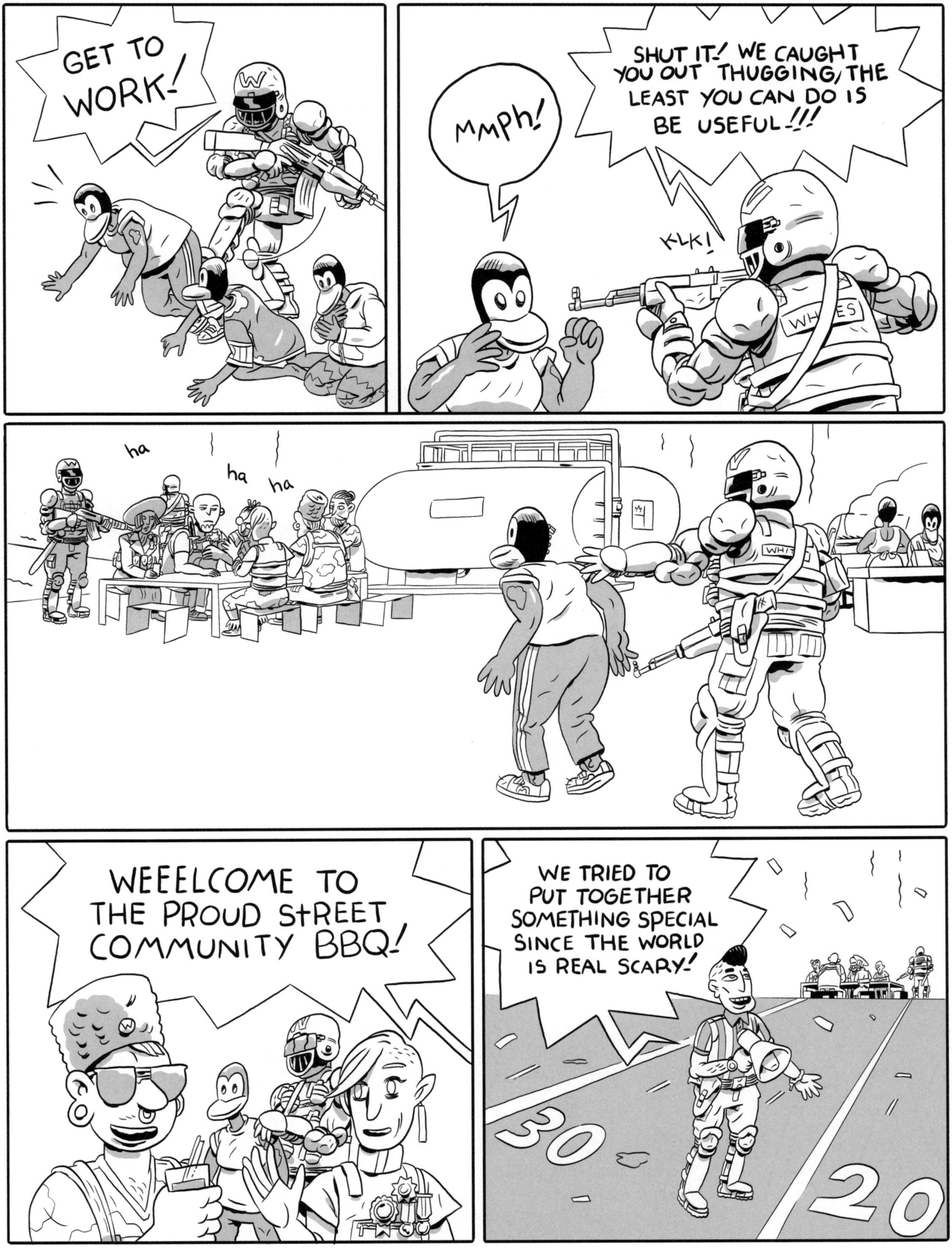
GET TO WORK!
MMPH!
SHUT IT! WE CAUGHT YOU OUT THUGGING, THE LEAST YOU CAN DO IS BE USEFUL!!!
KLK!
WHITES
ha
ha
ha
WHIT
WEEELCOME TO THE PROUD StREET COMMUNITY BBQ!
WE TRIED TO PUT TOGETHER SOMETHING SPECIAL SINCE THE WORLD IS REAL SCARY!
30
20

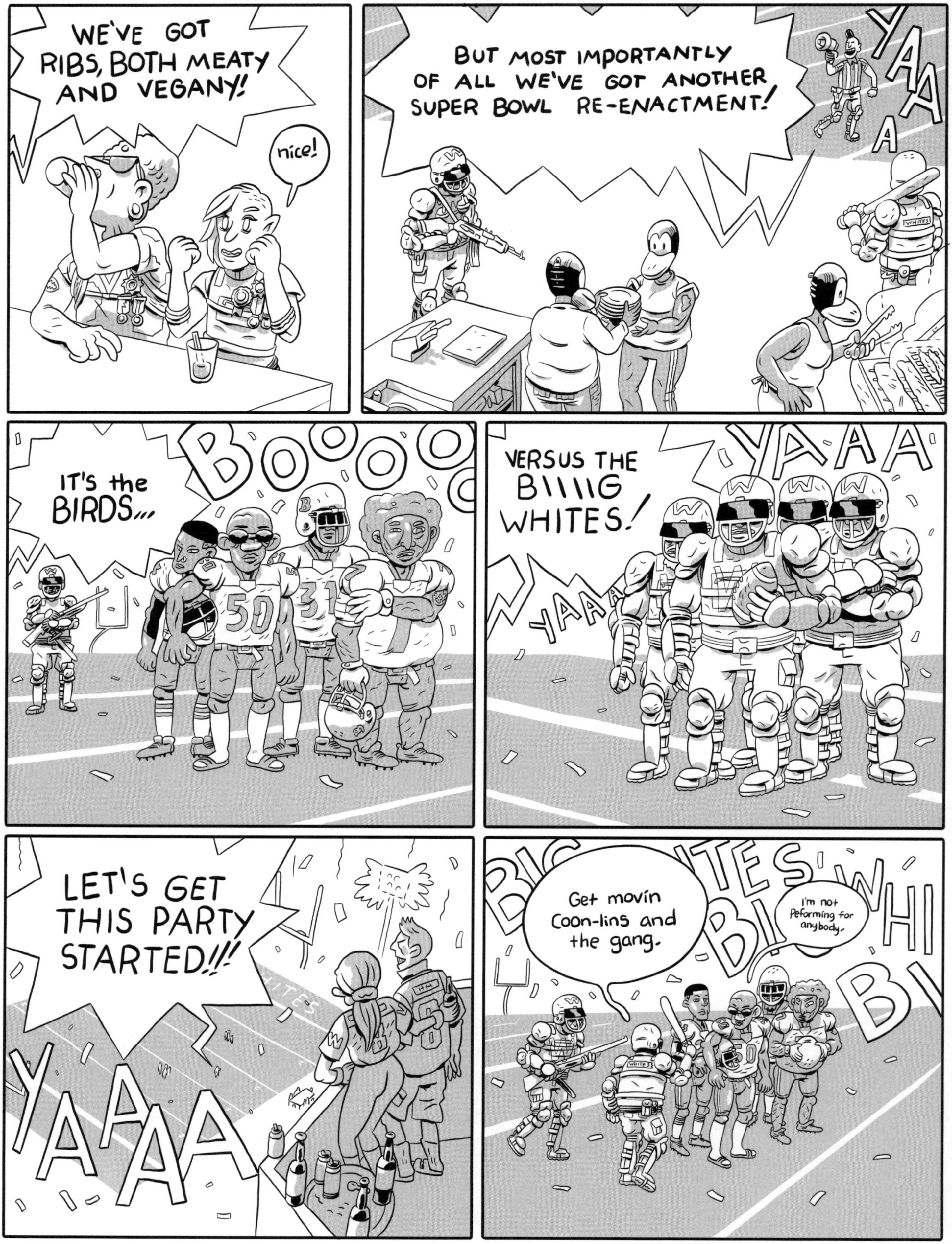
WE'VE GOT RIBS, BOTH MEATY AND VEGANY!
nice!
BUT MOST IMPORTANTLY OF ALL WE'VE GOT ANOTHER SUPER BOWL RE-ENACTMENT!
YAAAA
IT'S the BIRDS...
BOOOOO
VERSUS THE BIIIIG WHITES!
YAAAA
YAAAA
LET'S GET THIS PARTY STARTED!!!
YAAAA
Get movin Coon-lins and the gang.
I'm not Peforming for anybody.

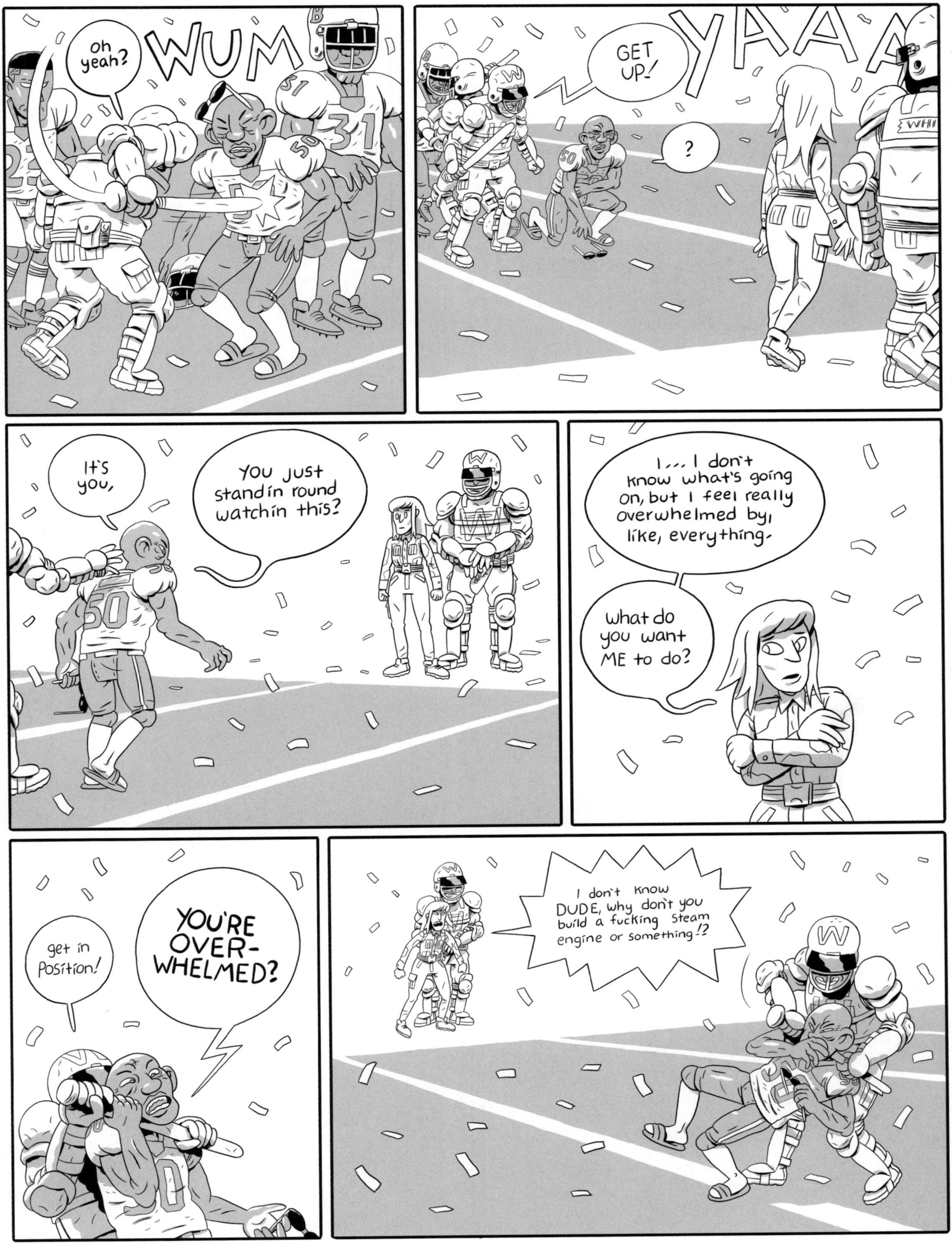
oh yeah?
WUM
GET UP!
YAAA
?
It's you,
You just standin round watchin this?
I... I don't know what's going on, but I feel really overwhelmed by, like, everything.
what do you want ME to do?
get in position!
YOU'RE OVER-WHELMED?
I don't know DUDE, why don't you build a fucking steam engine or something!?

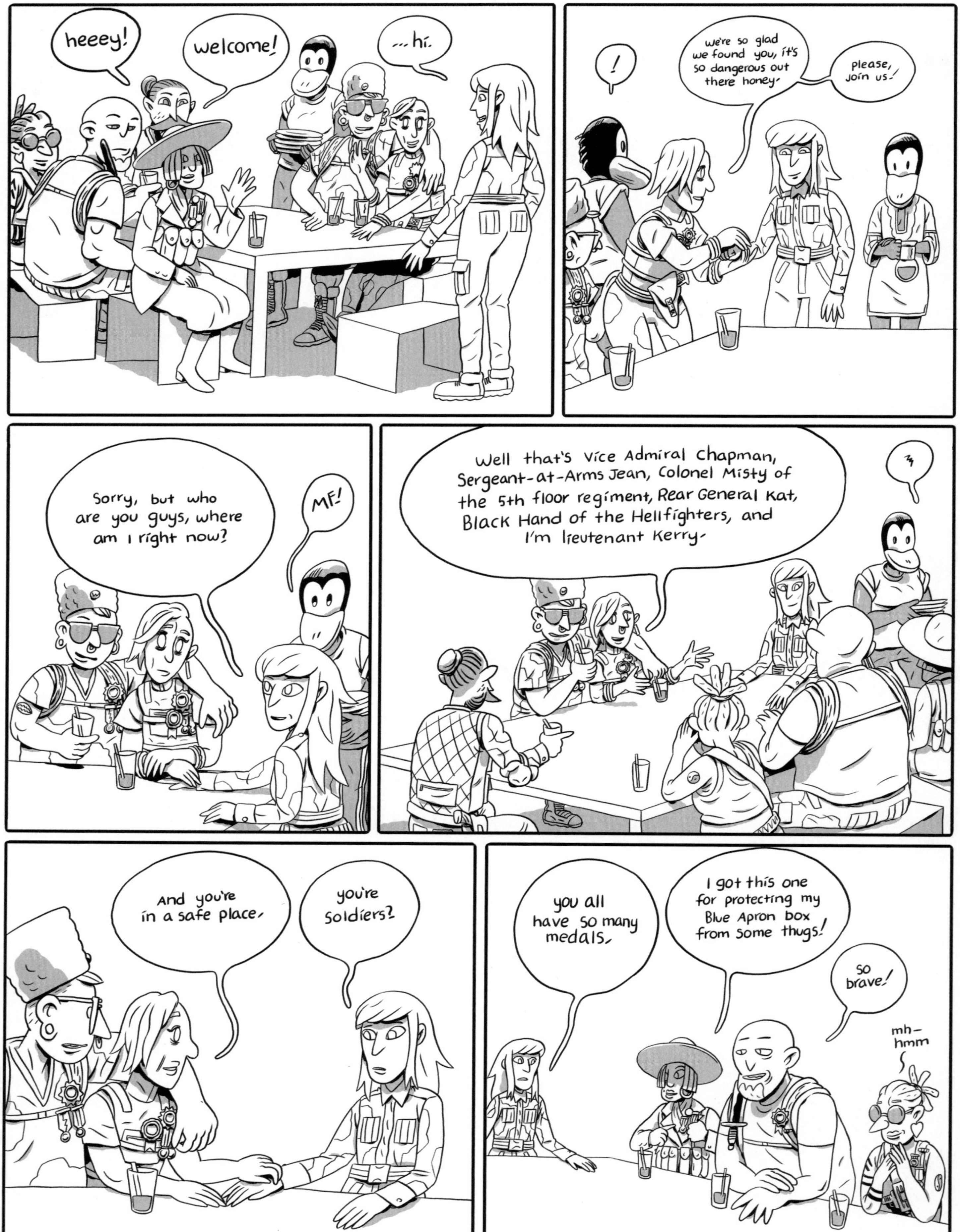
heeey!
welcome!
...hi.
!
We're so glad we found you, it's so dangerous out there honey.
please, join us.
Sorry, but who are you guys, where am I right now?
MF!
Well that's Vice Admiral Chapman, Sergeant-at-Arms Jean, Colonel Misty of the 5th floor regiment, Rear General Kat, Black Hand of the Hellfighters, and I'm lieutenant Kerry.
And you're in a safe place.
you're soldiers?
you all have so many medals.
I got this one for protecting my Blue Apron box from some thugs!
so brave!
mh-hmm

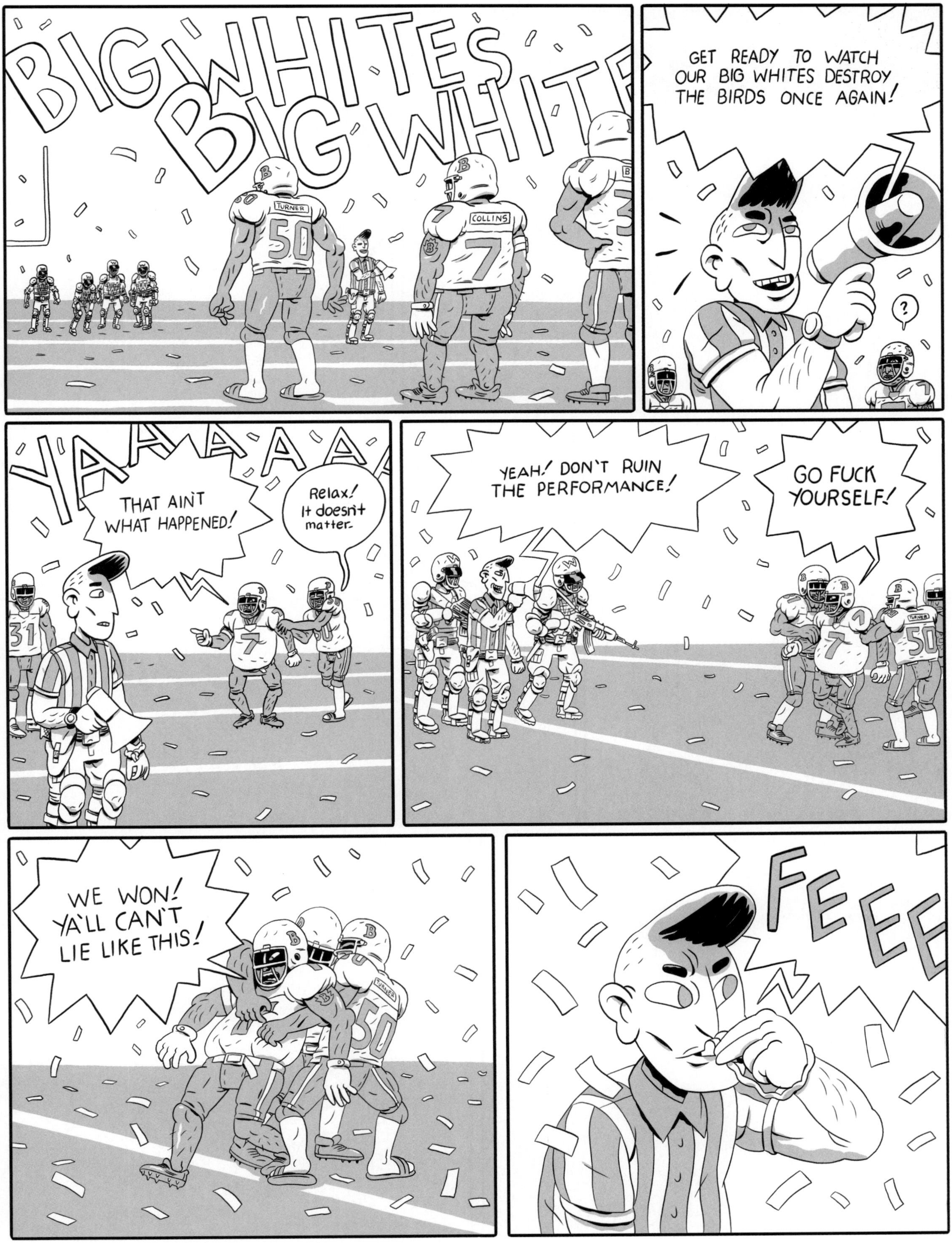
BIG WHITES
BIG WHITE
TURNER
50
COLLINS
7
GET READY TO WATCH OUR BIG WHITES DESTROY THE BIRDS ONCE AGAIN!
?
YAAAAA
THAT AIN'T WHAT HAPPENED!
Relax! It doesn't matter.
YEAH! DON'T RUIN THE PERFORMANCE!
GO FUCK YOURSELF!
WE WON! YA'LL CAN'T LIE LIKE THIS!
FEEE

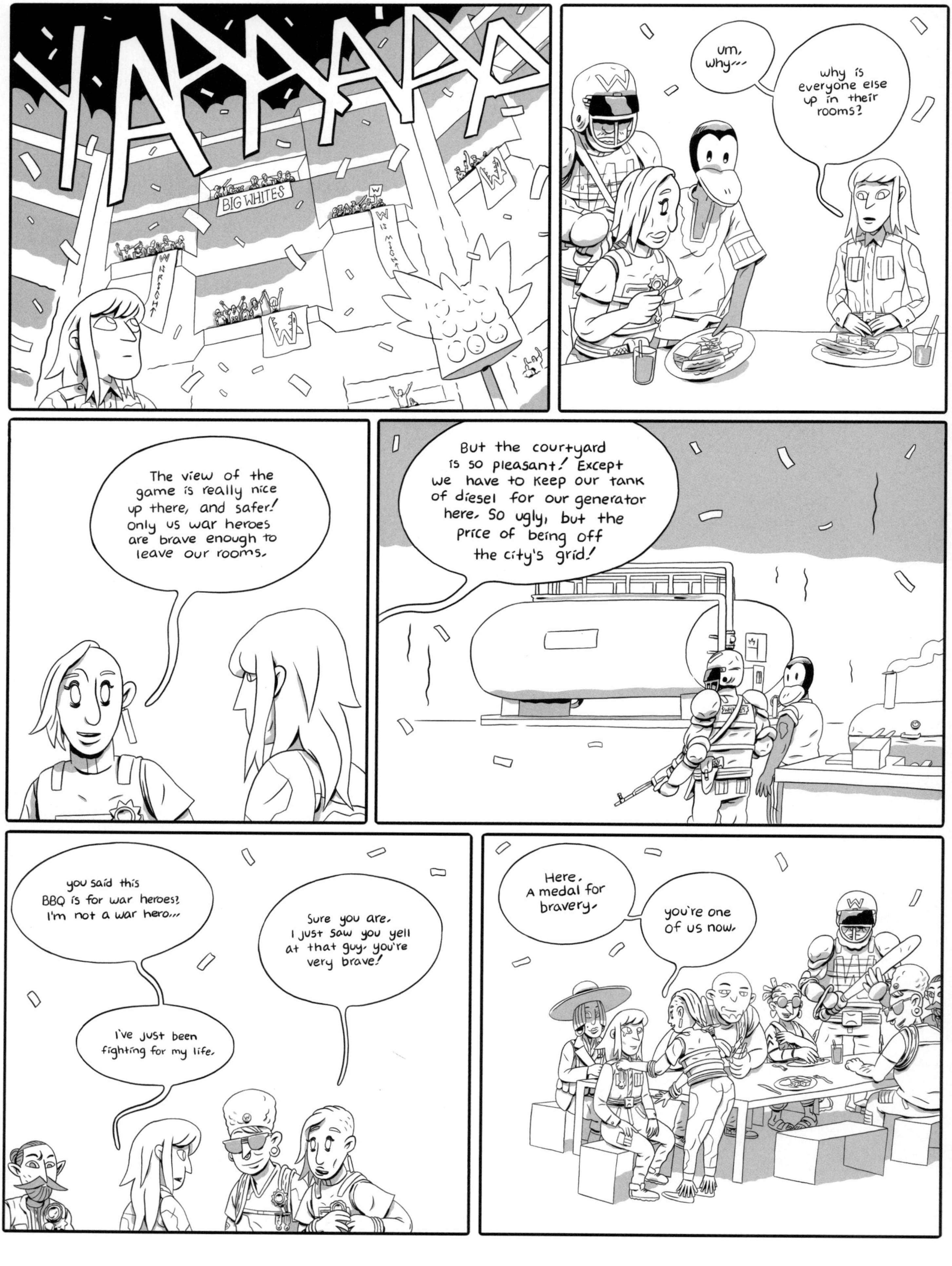
YAAAAAA
BIG WHITES
um, why...
why is everyone else up in their rooms?
The view of the game is really nice up there, and safer! only us war heroes are brave enough to leave our rooms.
But the courtyard is so pleasant! Except we have to keep our tank of diesel for our generator here. So ugly, but the price of being off the city's grid!
you said this BBQ is for war heroes? I'm not a war hero...
I've just been fighting for my life.
Sure you are. I just saw you yell at that guy, you're very brave!
Here. A medal for bravery.
you're one of us now.

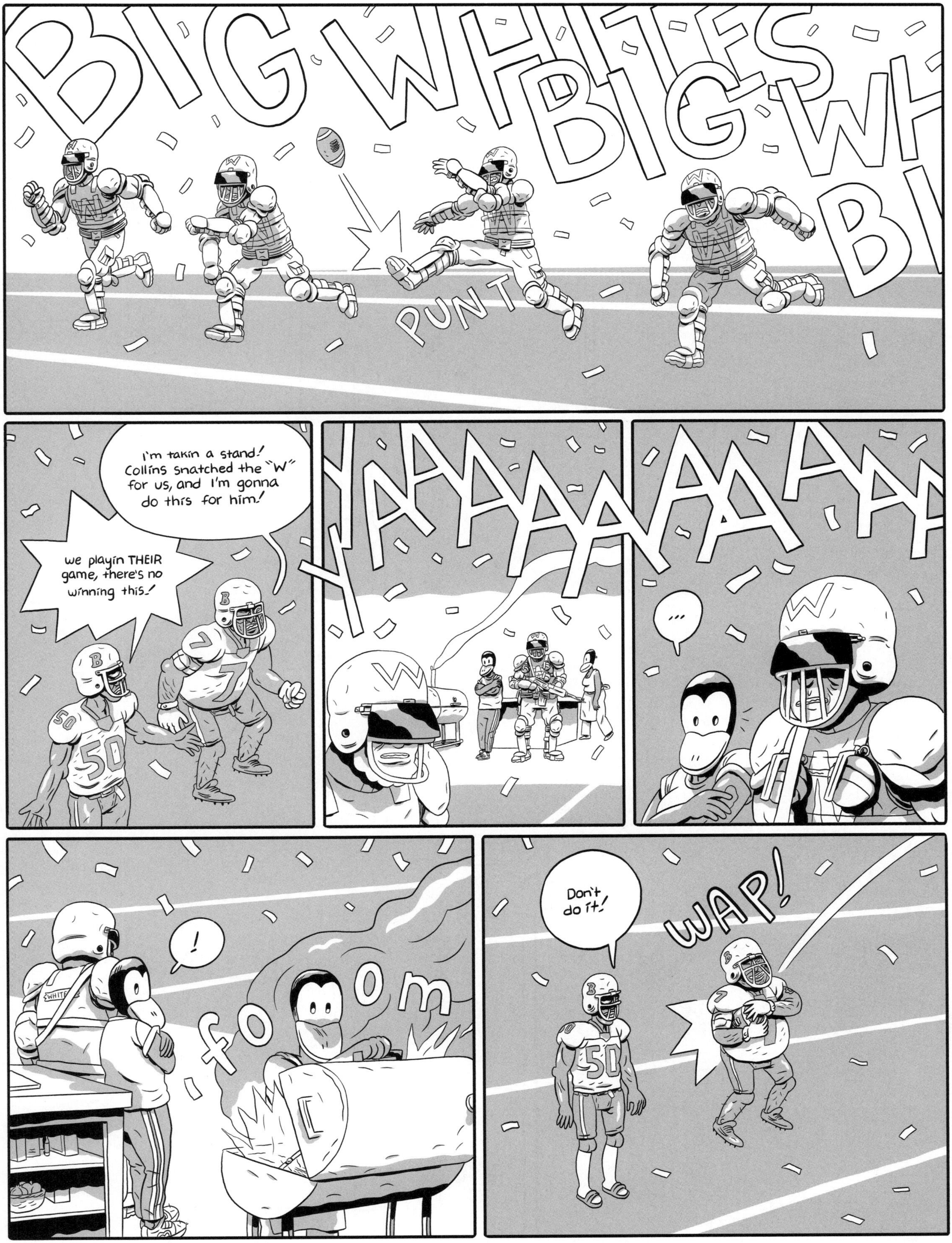
BIG WHITES BIG WH BI
PUNT
I'm takin a stand! Collins snatched the "W" for us, and I'm gonna do this for him!
we playin THEIR game, there's no winning this!
YAAAAAAAAAAAA
...
!
foom
Don't do it!
WAP!

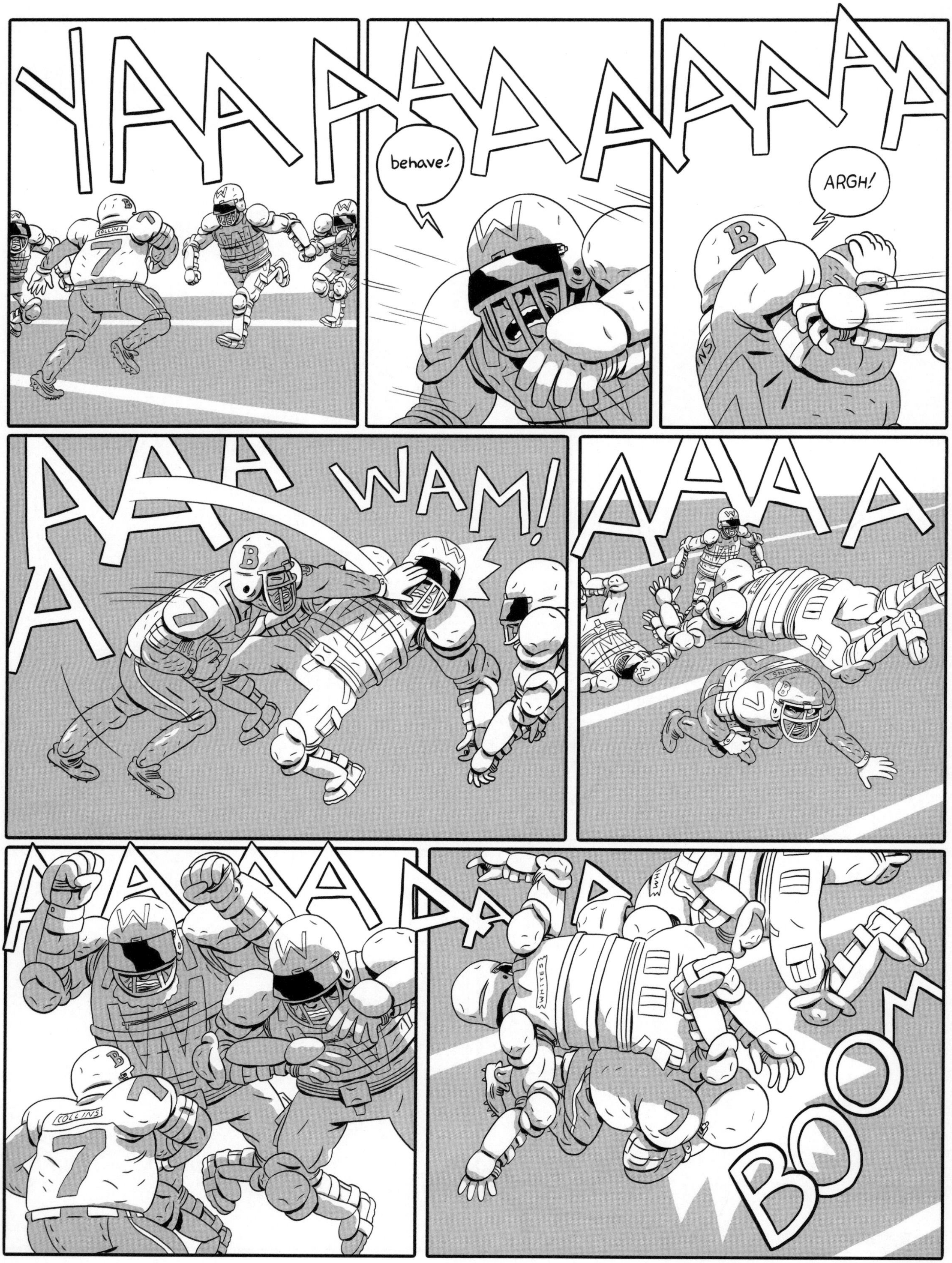
YAAAAAAAAAAA
behave!
ARGH!
COLLINS
AAAAA
WAM!
AAAA
AAAAA
WHITES
BOOM

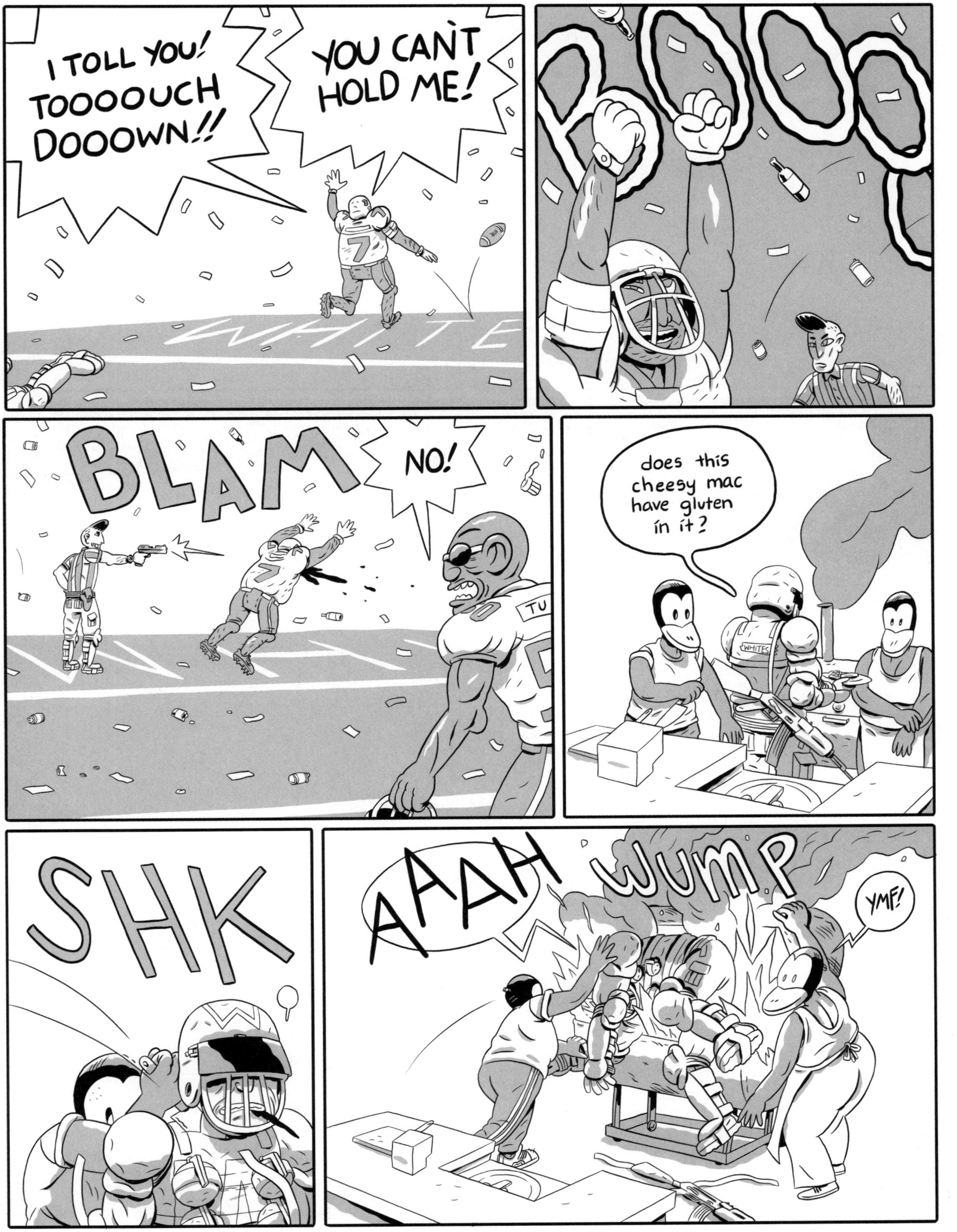
I TOLL YOU! TOOOOUCH DOOOWN!!
YOU CAN'T HOLD ME!
WHITE
BOOOOO
BLAM
NO!
TU
does this cheesy mac have gluten in it?
WHITES
SHK
AAAH
WUMP
YMF!

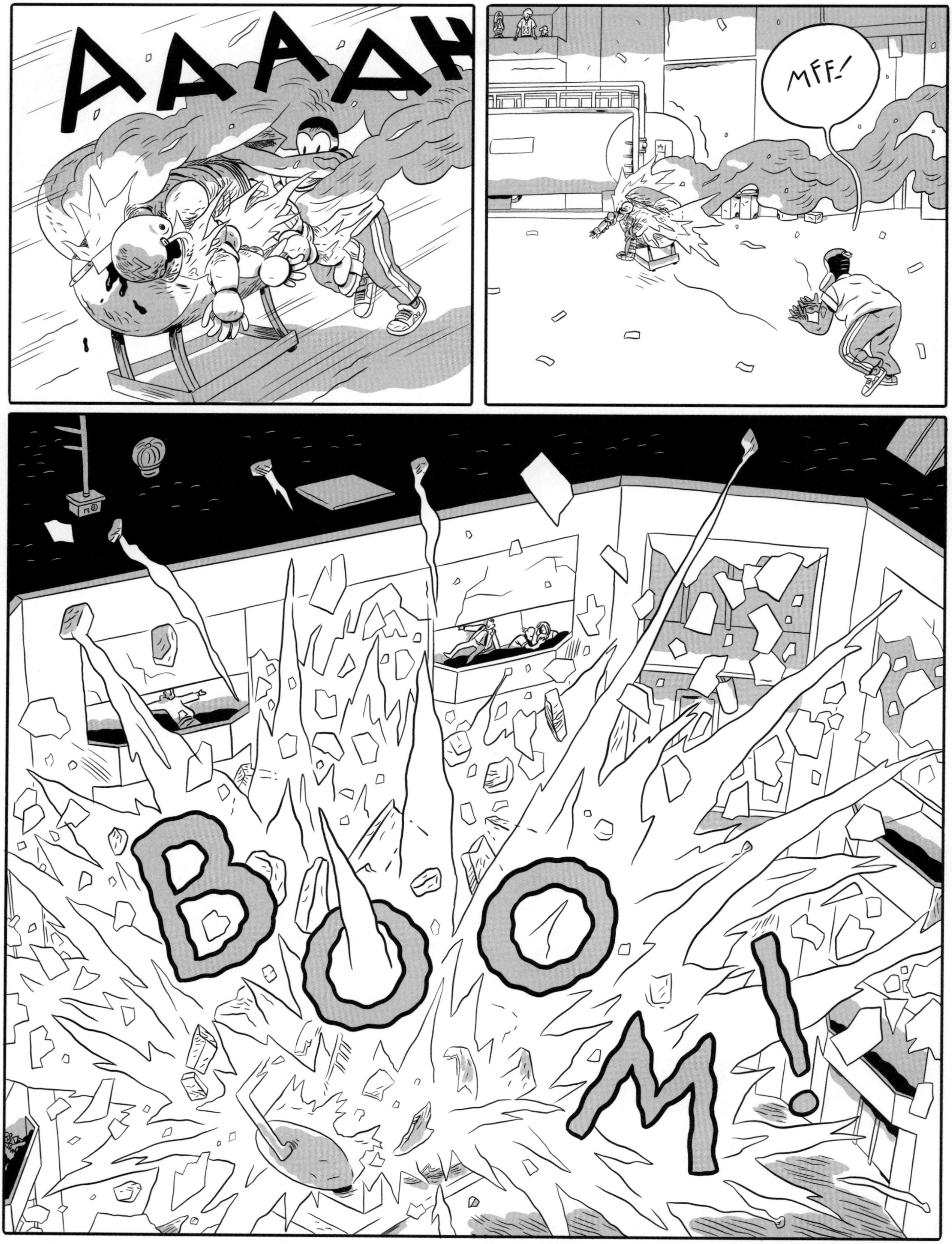
AAAH
MFF!
BOOM!

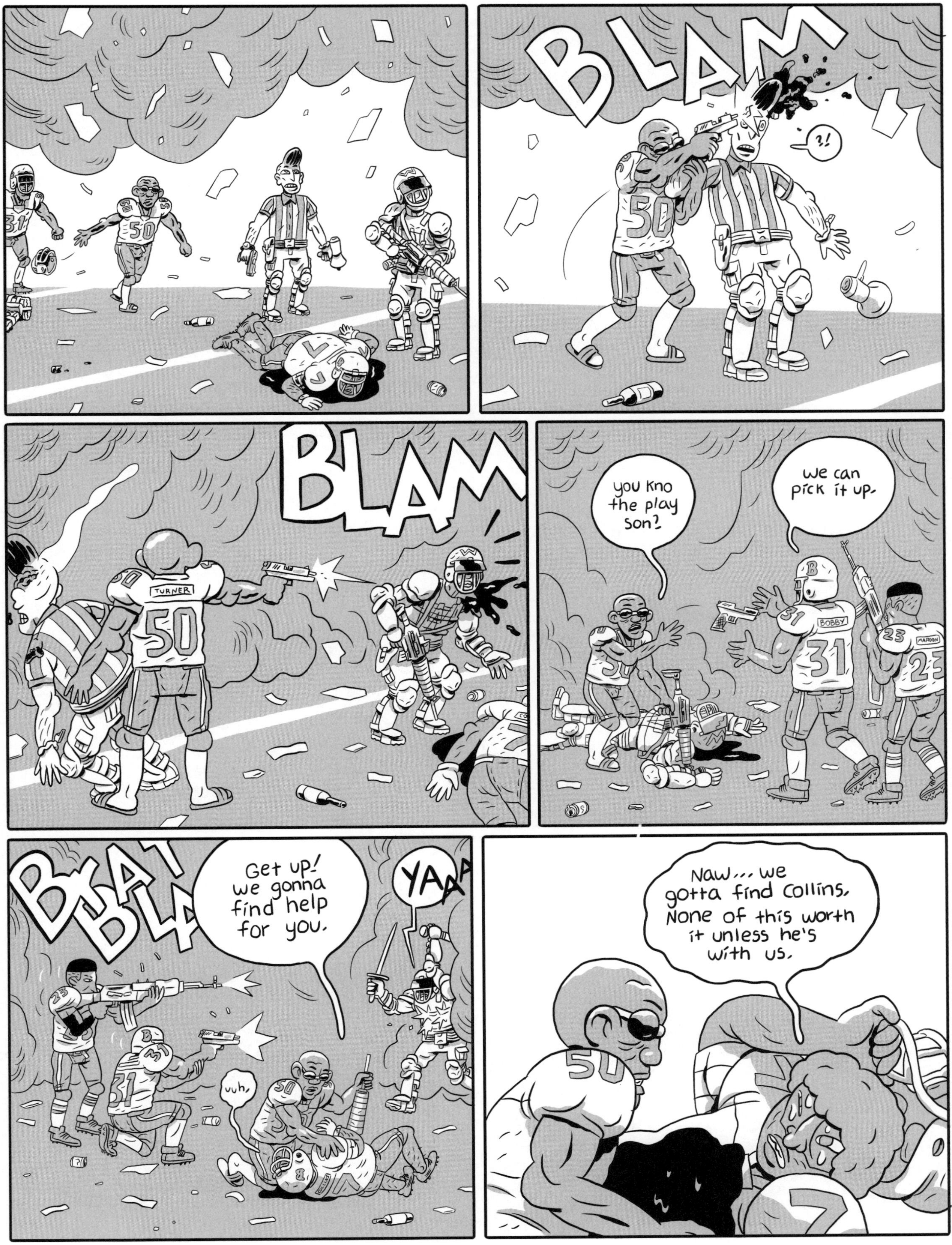
BLAM
?!
BLAM
TURNER
you kno the play son?
we can pick it up.
BOBBY
MAROON
BRAT
BLA
Get up! we gonna find help for you.
YAAA
uuh,
Naw... we gotta find Collins. None of this worth it unless he's with us.

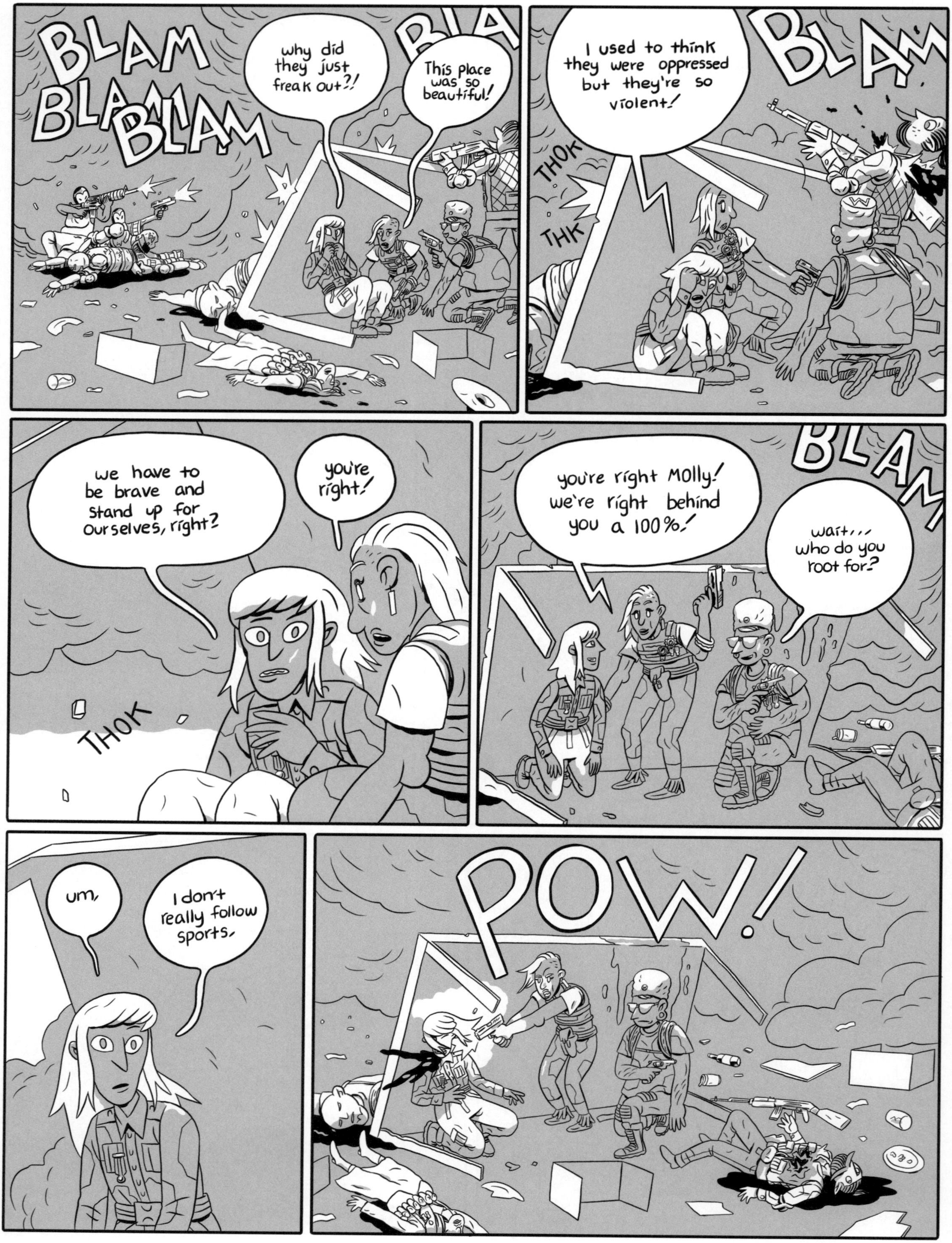
BLAM
BLAM BLAM
BLAM
why did they just freak out?!
BLA
This place was so beautiful!
I used to think they were oppressed but they're so violent!
BLAM
THOK
THK
we have to be brave and stand up for ourselves, right?
you're right!
THOK
BLAM
you're right Molly! we're right behind you a 100%!
wait... who do you root for?
um,
I don't really follow sports.
POW!

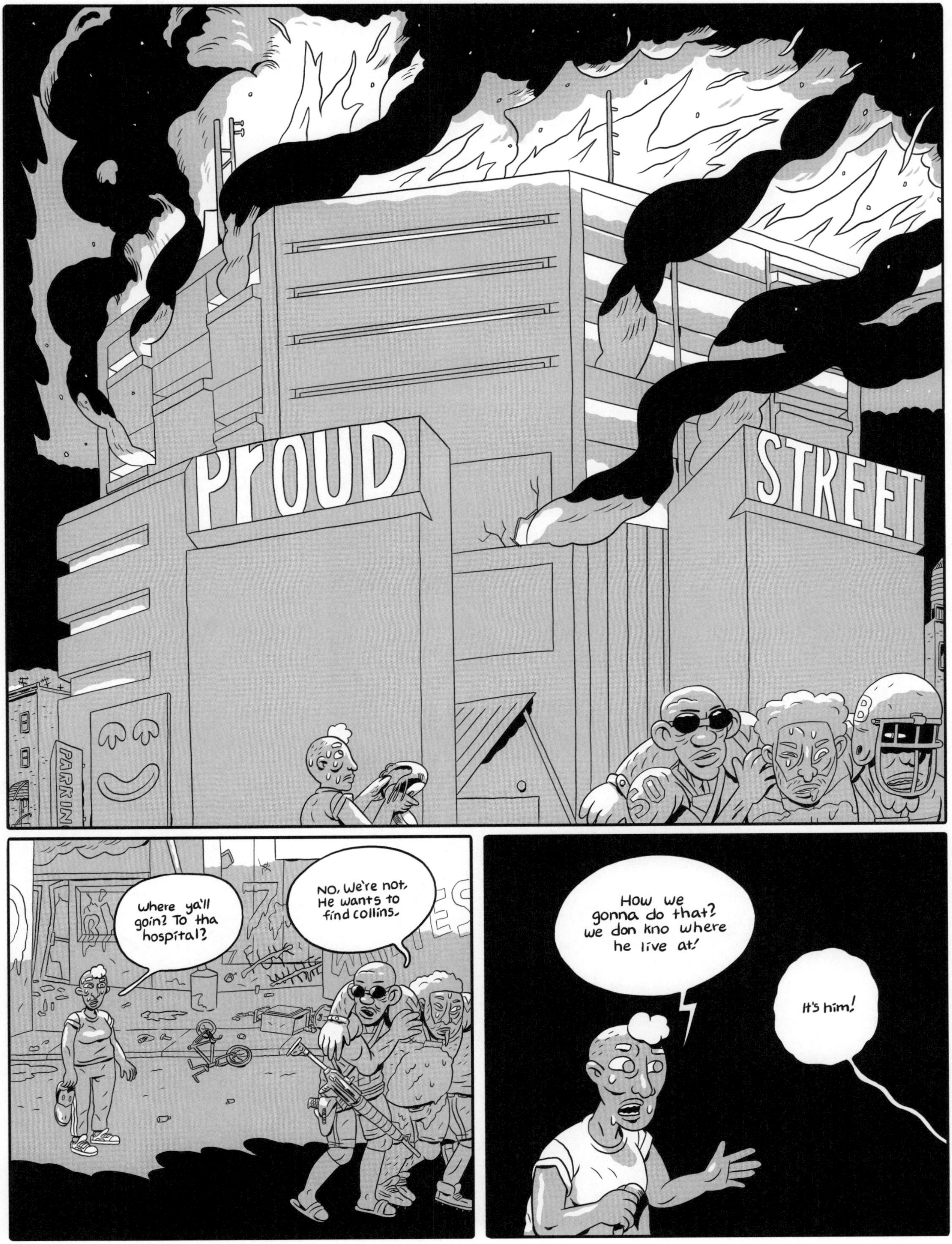

Proud
STREET
Where ya'll goin? To tha hospital?
NO, We're not, He wants to find collins.
How we gonna do that? we don kno where he live at!
It's him!

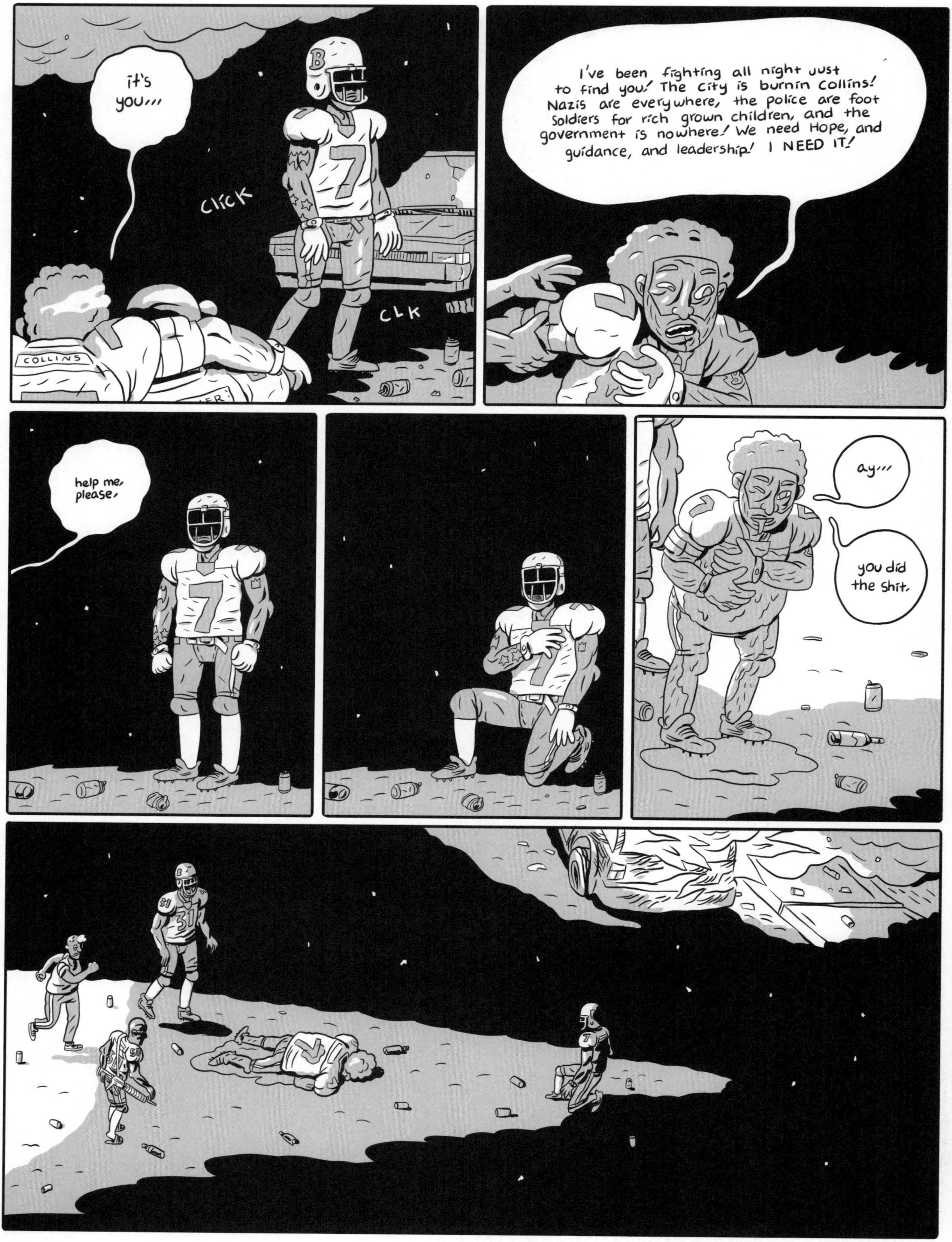

it's you...
CLICK
CLK
COLLINS
I've been fighting all night just to find you! The city is burnin Collins! Nazis are everywhere, the police are foot soldiers for rich grown children, and the government is nowhere! We need Hope, and guidance, and leadership! I NEED IT!
help me, please,
ay...
you did the shit.

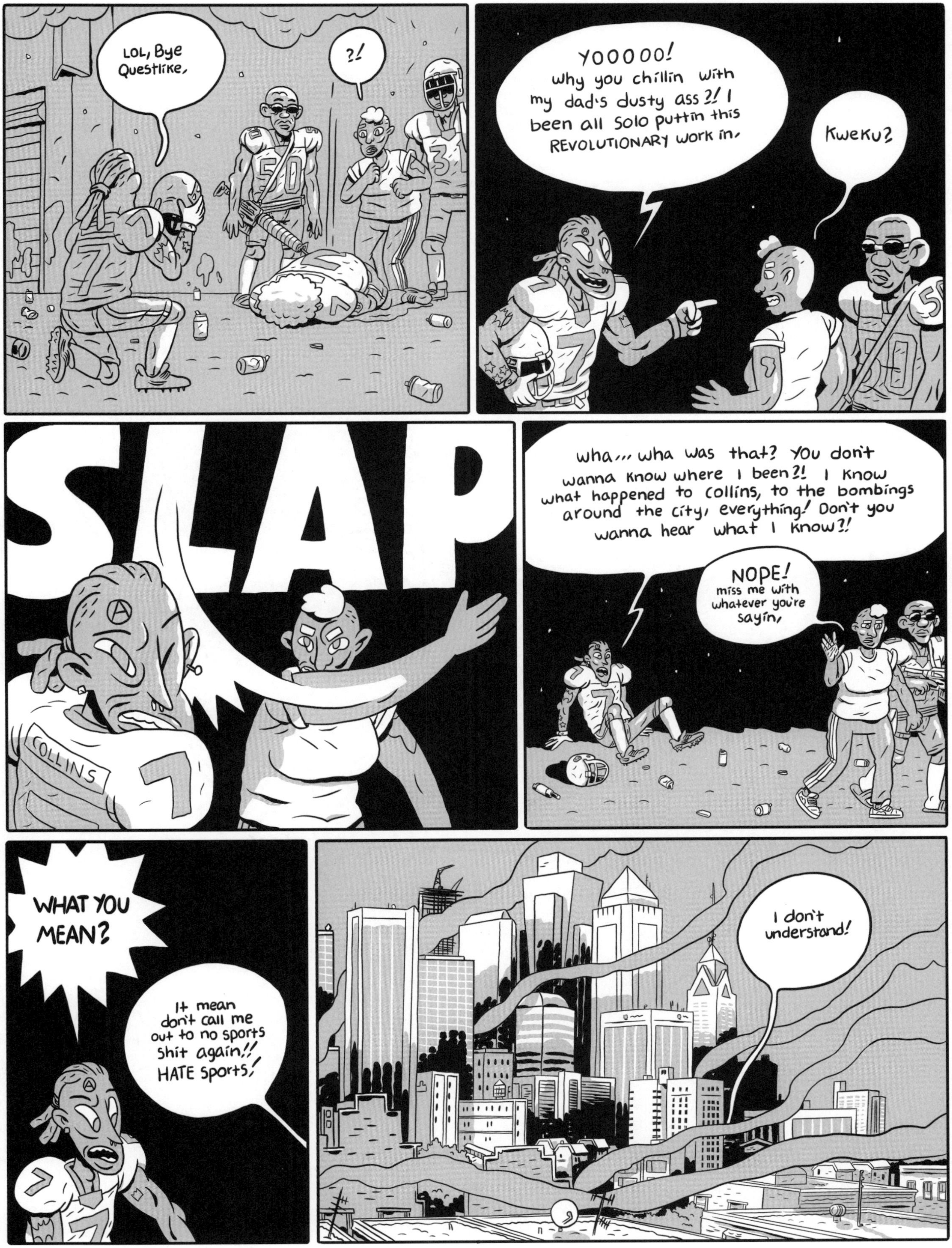
LOL, Bye Questlike,
?!
YOOOOO! Why you chillin with my dad's dusty ass?! I been all solo puttin this REVOLUTIONARY work in,
Kweku?
SLAP
COLLINS
wha... wha was that? You don't wanna know where I been?! I know what happened to Collins, to the bombings around the city, everything! Don't you wanna hear what I know?!
NOPE! miss me with whatever you're sayin,
WHAT YOU MEAN?
It mean don't call me out to no sports shit again!! HATE sports!
I don't understand!

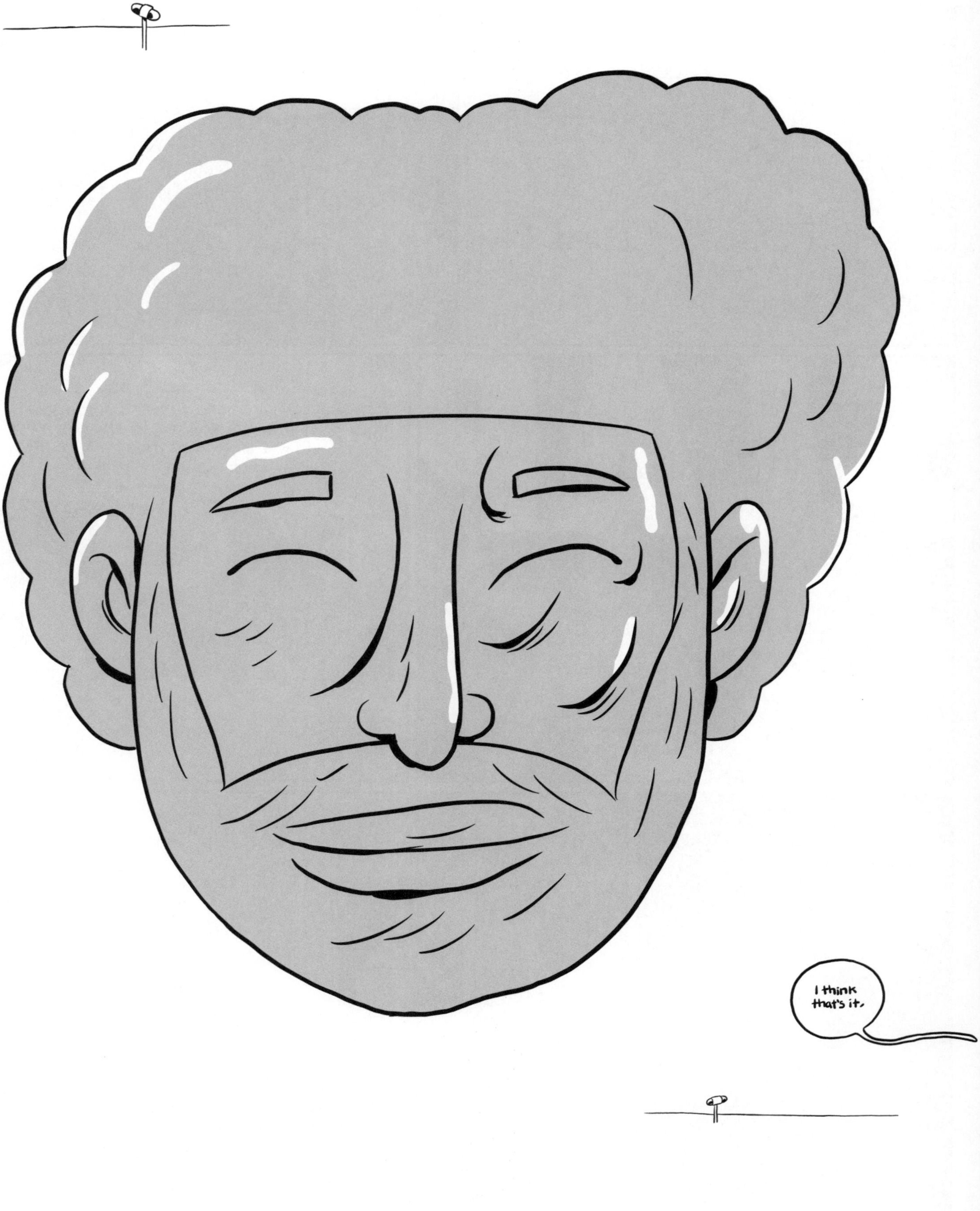
I think that's it.

Published by Koyama Press
Koyamapress.com

First edition- February 2020

ISBN- 978-1-927668-75-7

Printed in China